FINDING HOME
A Monastic Journey

D1744881

by

Dennis Berk CR

Mirfield Publications

Published in Great Britain in 2014 by Mirfield Publications
Community of the Resurrection
Stocksbank Road
Mirfield
West Yorkshire
WF14 0BN

www.monastery-stay.co.uk/shop

British Library Cataloguing in Publication Data. A catalogue record for this book is available from the British Library.

ISBN 978-0-902834-32-3

Table of Contents

Finding Home: *Preface*

To many modern minds, the Religious life seems both remote and unfathomable. With ideas formed only by the superficial interpretations found in television dramas and even comedy films, it is understandable that popular misconceptions abound. Monks, nuns, friars and sisters are unusual figures, dressed in strange clothes, their way of life difficult to understand. Even to those who are churchgoers, Religious life can be puzzling. So if someone today hears of a friend or relative intending to join a community, the reaction is usually a blank expression of surprise before asking the question 'why?'.

Yet Religious life is still a very significant component of what makes the Church. The impulse to lead the Christian life in an intense and particular way has been a part of the Church's witness from early in its history. It has taken many forms and has ebbed and flowed with respect to numbers over the generations. Yet, even denominations created at the Reformation, whose founding identity included the rejection of monastic life, eventually found vocations to such a life impossible to deny. Among Anglicans, there were hints and glimpses of such through several centuries until in the nineteenth century a full revival took root.

But, the contemporary mind asks, is this life still significant in the twenty-first century? How does a person come to enter a Religious community when brought up in modern western society with its emphasis on individualism and consumerism? In this book, Father Dennis Berk shares with us his own journey exploring a vocation leading to profession in the Community of the Resurrection. Yet this is more than a personal memoir. The author weaves amongst the facts of his own life thoughts and reflections on the reasons for the Religious life. He explores how a person moves towards discovering all that the life entails and how a decision to try a vocation enfolds. After entering the novitiate, there are the stresses of abandoning the individualism and consumerism with which he had been surrounded since childhood.

The stages on his formation as a monk may be particular to the Religious life but they also echo the challenges that many find in the Christian life. All Christians have to struggle against accumulating possessions, the temptations of being selfish in relationships and the need to recognise authority outside our own self-will. Living in community in the wider sense is something modern-day Christians have to take seriously and re-discover anew in every generation. The presence of Religious life in the Church challenges us to do that. So this book is more than a personal story. It gives each reader a question to which to respond. Dare we embrace our own Christian vocation - wherever it leads?

Dr Petà Dunstan
Fellow, St Edmund's College, Cambridge
Editor of Anglican Religious Life Year Book

Chapter 1 : Asking "Why?"

"Why do you want to be a monk?" That question was put to me countless times throughout the course of my last few months in parish ministry. It was voiced as I was conducting my priestly duties whilst packing up my worldly goods in preparation for moving out of the rectory and relocating overseas. *"Will your robe be yellow or brown?"* some people asked as images of Hare Krishna devotees or a rustic St. Francis of Assisi filled their thoughts. Clearly people found it rather bizarre, and maybe even abnormal, for me to be embarking on such an unusual journey into the seemingly exotic and secretive world of a monastery.

Sometimes the repetition of that question, though asked from a sincere concern for my welfare, tempted me with the mischievous desire to respond with the retort *"Why not?"* However I think that I refrained from uttering that response to what was an expression of genuine interest in my motivations for pursuing a vocational call that is counter-cultural to society's understanding of a successful career.

One reason for my embarrassment by that question was due to my frustration in conveying an intelligent response. Despite my earnest longing to follow Christ by responding to this call that was laid upon my heart, I felt that I was not adequately expressing the powerful motivations that were summoning me to give up so many significant aspects of the world in which I was comfortably ensconced. How could I provide a rationale to explain why I was choosing to embrace a monastic lifestyle? When asked *"Why do you want to be a monk?"* my struggle was for a response conveying the intensity of the desires that were compelling me to pursue this particular life calling.

That question was a good one to ask, and I am glad that the curiosity of people prompted them to address that enquiry to me because it challenged me to probe for an answer. Initially I was discomfited at not being able to produce a wise and witty response encapsulating the profound spiritual merits of the monastic life. But I benefited by being driven to explore monasticism more deeply so that I could articulate a response to the question *"Why be a monk?"*

Despite now having spent some time living the monastic life, I have to confess that the monastic vocation remains deeply mysterious and not fully comprehensible to me. Several years have passed since I walked through the iron gates that provide entrance to the grounds occupied by the Community of the Resurrection, yet I still find it difficult to articulate the nature of this life within a "cloistered" world that is largely unknown and misunderstood by society. However one thing I know with certainty is that at the heart of my life in this monastery is the desire to embrace God's love and his call to discover my true self.

I still have a limited vantage point from which to examine monasticism because I've only been living here since the autumn of 2009. Furthermore I cannot predict the future development or the eventual progression of my ongoing journey with this community of monks. All that I can do is convey something about my experiences up to the present moment. So this is an account of the journey that I am making in quest of my heart's desire as each day I am engaged in travelling one step closer to my spiritual home.

When a person expresses an intention to enter a monastery, a common response that I've observed in people hearing this news is wide-eyed shock and open-mouthed amazement. The thought of someone voluntarily choosing to "give up everything" and "leave the world," with all of its comforts and pleasures, can be very perplexing to understand. This difficulty of comprehension is exasperated by the misconceptions of religious life that exist within society. Images of extreme ascetical rigours are visualised as occurring within a context of medieval primitivism. Some of the portrayals of nuns and monks that have been fed to the public by Hollywood have reinforced this by showing the cloistered life as intrinsically warped and unhealthy. Maybe it is these media-induced images lodged in our minds, showing scenes of a monastic milieu characterised by an unworldly fanaticism, that are unsettling people and leading them to ask the "why" question about a monastic vocation?

It was my efforts to answer that question, and to break down the stereotypes that skew people's impressions of contemporary monks and nuns, that motivated me to write this book. Especially near and dear to me are the members of my family who have felt most intimately the physical absence that was the result of my removal from their midst when I relocated overseas to a monastic community. But this book also is directed to anyone who questions why someone would pursue such a peculiar pathway of Christian service. From the beginning of setting out to write this book I wanted it to be applicable to people who are asking questions, striving to know God's will, seeking to follow their heart's desire, and journeying on a quest to find their soul's true home.

When a person voices aloud a plan to pursue a monastic vocation, and then follows through with that pursuit by joining a religious community, it is easy to make the mistake of thinking that their desired goal and final destination have been reached. This is not true. Even after making a formal commitment by taking vows the consummation of the journey to their spiritual home still has not been attained. All that they've done is to embark upon a pathway on which they will travel for the rest of their life. I have discovered that it is not a comfortable pathway. This is because it is a life that is very real and not a blissful fantasy. But within the cloistered life there is the profound peace and the deep security of being held in the intimate embrace of God's unfailing love.

My exploration of this pathway commenced quite a few years before I arrived at the gates of the monastery to "test the waters" for this unique vocational journey. Whilst still a little child this journey began for me with an awareness of God's abiding love, and its origins are rooted firmly within the first home that God gave me: my biological family. It was in that nurturing context that I was taught the Christian faith by my devout parents whose own unstinting love has shown me an example of how to love myself, to love other people, and to love God. Although I still struggle with loving, at least I am fortunate in having been blessed with such good role models.

My original reasons for joining the Community of the Resurrection have changed as my vocation has matured, and now whenever people ask what motivated me to become a monk the answer that first comes to mind is a simple one word response: "Love." Only a deep longing to love God with every possible ounce of passion could have led me into the monastic life and sustained my journey to this day. It is through love that God is known. Our wounded nature is made whole by love which brings us closer to God. In order to meet and commune with God we must entrust ourselves unconditionally to his love. The prime intent of monks and nuns is to immerse ourselves completely in God's love.

Essential components of love are self-offering and striving for intimacy and unity, which apply not only to our relationship with God but also to our relationships with people. Speaking of this interplay between human and divine love, St. Bernard, a medieval abbot of

Clairvaux, wrote that God "...is the initiator of our love and its final goal. He is himself the occasion of human love; he gives us the power to love, and brings our desire to consummation.... His love for us opens up inside of us the way to love, and is the reward of our own reaching out in love."[1] Although I fall far short in giving and receiving love as God intends, none the less I am immersed in God's love at every moment of my life.

A Prayer for Vocations petitions Christ to "kindle in the hearts of men and women the desire to follow you in the Religious life. Give to those whom you call grace ... to make the whole-hearted surrender which you ask, and for love of you to persevere to the end."[2] The kindling of the vocational fire that compelled me to pursue this counter-cultural pathway was not the warm, cosy glow of a well-controlled hearthside fire. Instead I've found it to involve the searing pain and the uncomfortable burning of being consumed in an immolation of the self. Fortunately I've also seen evidence of how God's grace enables new life to arise from amidst the ashes of our old selfish natures. Engaging in a whole-hearted surrender to God is a frightening enterprise to undertake. As I have become vulnerable by opening up to love the painful reconstruction work of my transformation has begun to occur.

I do not like being a building site because internal upheaval is disconcerting, and I am not fond of having my orderly plans thrown into disarray by the movement of the Spirit. One reason for saying that prayer for vocations in my devotions is due to my recognition of how reluctantly I bare my entire self in surrendering my whole heart to God. This is why daily I send heavenwards a petition for help to persevere in loving God and all the rest of God's creation in whom the divine image is reflected. Living for God is choosing to love, which is not easy because living out love cannot be done in some esoteric manner directed to an abstract entity. It takes place within the interactions and relationships that we have with the flesh and blood reality of the actual persons whom we meet face to face in daily life.

More than a dozen years ago I began to make serious enquiries about the monastic life. As the twenty-first century commenced I made my first visit to Mirfield and immediately found myself attracted to the

---

[1] Celebrating the Saints: Daily Spiritual Readings. Ed. Robert Atwell, p. 291.
[2] Anglican Religious Life, 2010-2011 edition, p. vii.

love that was evident in the members of this particular religious community in northern England. Then I began the probationary year that precedes admission as an oblate of the Community of the Resurrection. For those unfamiliar with that term, an 'oblate' is defined as: "Someone associated closely with a community, but who will be living a modified form of the Rule which allows him or her to live outside the Religious house. Oblates are so-called because they make an oblation (offering) of obedience to the community instead of taking the profession vows."[3] My admission as an oblate provided me with the opportunity to develop a significant connection with a monastic community, and over the course of the next eight years I continued exploring the vocational desire that was growing steadily within my heart.

As an oblate I was not residing in the monastery, yet I was able to continue the process of learning more about this way of life. For nearly a decade this association nourished my soul as I visited and corresponded with them, and my desire to live with them kept on increasing. Finally the constancy and the intensity of my longing compelled me to initiate the formal enquiries necessary for seeking admission.

Despite my eagerness and my desire to become a monk, it was not easy for me to sever the emotional, familial, occupational, and logistical links that I had to break in order to relocate overseas and enter religious life. The passing of each year spent in association with the Community of the Resurrection witnessed my heart yearning more and more to join them. However I remained anxious about taking the final step that would remove me from the comfortable familiarity of everyday existence as I knew it. Was I really ready to plunge into a world that would entail a dramatic re-arrangement of all aspects of my life?

I still recall the feelings of sadness that weighed upon me as I bid farewell to the various members of my family. There was some degree of excitement held out by the prospect of discovering myself within a context and culture different from anything that I'd known before, but even my anticipation at the stimulating possibilities held out before me was not enough to overcome every reservation that I harboured within myself. I was reaching forward with anticipation yet I was filled with

---

[3] Ibid., p. 189.

fear about embracing this new life with all of the discipline that a communal existence entails. Amidst my anxieties I found myself echoing other people's words as I asked myself *"Why do I want to become a monk?"*

Seen from the vantage point of that juncture in time, the pursuit of a monastic vocation appeared to be a forbidding enterprise for which to uproot myself from all that was comfortingly familiar in order to respond to God's call. Surely I could serve God just as well by remaining in parish ministry? Couldn't I continue to be a servant of God as a priest settled successfully in a church amongst parishioners who liked me? These were questions weighing on my mind as I said goodbye to my parents. Later when I sat gazing out the window of the airplane as it departed from New York's John F. Kennedy airport, there were so many conflicting emotions coursing through me that I wondered whether I had deluded myself into falsely discerning a divine summons to the monastic life.

I know that I'm not the only person to have experienced such reservations. It is natural to have some hesitation when venturing into new avenues of ministry. Even an apostle of such considerable certitude as Saint Paul recognised that there is an opaque quality to the spiritual journey which may cause our steps to be a bit hesitant or faltering at times. In his letter to the Corinthians, Saint Paul makes the acknowledgement that "For now we see in a mirror dimly, but then we shall see face to face. Now I know only in part, then I will know fully, even as I have been fully known." [4]

In those emotionally wrenching moments when I was making my departure from the terra firma of North America, I was seeing only dimly the pathway of my vocational journey into monasticism. One of the reasons that I was looking forward to arriving at Mirfield was my expectation that once ensconced there I would be enveloped by an undeniable vocational certainty. I hoped that this would provide irrefutable clarity and a great spiritual vision that would dispel all of my anxieties and doubts. But if the truth is told, then I must confess that even now I still only see rather dimly this spiritual pilgrimage upon which I am travelling.

I cannot claim an ability to see the whole expansive picture. Instead what I am discovering is that God enables me to see only the amount

---

[4] 1 Corinthians 13:12

that is necessary to continue walking upon this journey. For this reason, even though sometimes I find myself questioning "why," yet I can keep moving forward despite seeing things partially. Questions still arise but I am able to continue travelling on this monastic journey because I have the confidence of knowing that God is guiding my footsteps as I walk closer towards the light and love of Christ.

Chapter 2: Discerning the Best Match

Selecting the right religious community in which to test a vocation is much like choosing a life partner. Typically one dates several persons – usually not simultaneously – as part of the process of determining if a specific individual is the person with whom one feels enough romantic attraction, emotional harmony, and shared convictions that promise at least a hope for future domestic fulfilment and satisfaction. So too an aspirant to monasticism oftentimes has engaged in a process of visiting multiple monasteries in order to acquire a feel for the unique charism and distinctive ethos of each community. This was my personal experience. As part of my exploration of the attraction that I felt towards the monastic life, I'd visited several other abbeys and priories in the United States, Canada and England before finally deciding upon the Community of the Resurrection as the best match for me.

Perhaps it is not surprising that I shopped around before making my formal application for admission to Mirfield. As an American, born in a nation known worldwide for its embrace of consumerism, such an activity of "comparison shopping" could be regarded as an innate part of my character. However I do not want to give the impression that I approached this with a cavalier attitude of a-la-carte selectivity as though my choice was of no more significance than mulling over which cake to select from a buffet table spread with an array of desserts. Visiting several religious orders was more than a marketplace strategy of weighing each monastery and its members by comparison with their peers elsewhere. It was more like the journey that one makes into the solemn commitment of holy matrimony. There you have to arrive at a confident certainty of exchanging vows with the right person to whom you can unite in committed lifelong companionship. Similarly I entered this community with a hope that this will be a relationship lasting for the rest of my life.

Back in the autumn of 2002 it was necessary for me to travel to England to attend a ceremony of admission as an oblate of the Community of the Resurrection. Wanting to combine that visit with an opportunity for a holiday, I booked accommodations upon the *Queen Elizabeth 2* for a transatlantic crossing. That venerable liner made regular forays between the ports of New York and Southampton, and the *Cunard Line* that owned the ship promised six days of pleasure as conveyed in their advertisements which exclaimed: "Getting there is half the fun!"

Shortly after boarding, the orientation speeches delivered by members of the crew made it clear that I had embarked upon a "crossing" and not a "cruise." Unlike the routes that are plied by ships in the warm waters of the Caribbean or the Mediterranean, the *QE2* was steaming directly across the Atlantic to arrive in Britain without stopping at any intervening ports. This ship was not cruising around aimlessly from one tropical port to another as a leisurely way to spend a week of sightseeing. Instead, as its bow cut cleanly through the waves, it was forging ahead in a non-stop voyage towards a specific destination that was far beyond anything visible upon the horizon.

Upon reflection I see that transatlantic crossing aboard the *QE2* as providing an analogy for my journey of monastic discernment as that ship took me towards my destination in the West Yorkshire town of Mirfield. After having spent some years "cruising" through a variety of other religious orders, I'd come to a decision that the Community of the Resurrection was the one which I wanted to join. Now I was embarked upon a journey to a specific destination. No longer was I randomly roaming about on the seas of vocational indecision. Now I was committed to making a trip that would bring me to the brethren amongst whom I felt could be found a spiritual home.

Since the majority of contemporary travellers now traverse the gap between the European and the North American continents by spending some hours aboard a jet as it hurtles through the skies, most people do not have first-hand experience of what it is like to be aboard a ship crossing the Atlantic Ocean. For five days there is no sight of land and the only thing visible on the horizon is a seemingly endless expanse of water. As I stood there on deck leaning against the railing on the *QE2,* gazing at the vastness of the ocean, my mind recalled once having read in a science textbook that the water upon the earth today is all of the water that ever has existed. Upon a molecular level the sum total of the earth's water resources have not changed since the beginning of creation because the water cycle purifies and re-employs the very same water over and over again.

The thought came to me that the water upon which I was travelling is, in its elemental essence, the same as that over which God's spirit moved at the dawn of creation. Whilst standing there contemplating this it was necessary to grip the railing tightly. Even though the ship

11

was large and luxurious yet it was moving and shifting precariously beneath my feet. The *QE2* was not making a summertime voyage through placid seas in tropical climes. Instead it was crossing the Atlantic as the stormy month of November commenced. This feeling of being tossed about on the ocean called to mind the lyrics of Charlotte Elliott's hymn *"Just as I am, without one plea."* These are the words to the third verse of her hymn:

> Just as I am, tho' tossed about
> With many a conflict, many a doubt,
> Fightings within, and fears without,
> O Lamb of God, I come![5]

Later that same day I strolled down to the Queen's Room, one of several lounges aboard the *QE2*. There I enjoyed afternoon tea served with traditional British flare. Due to the sizeable waves buffeting the ship during this autumnal crossing, tea became a challenging experience of balancing cups and saucers as the liner rolled from side to side upon the high seas. Those not blessed with quick reflexes enabling them to respond adroitly to the unexpected pitch of the ship soon discovered that their china had slid off the table and into their laps or onto the floor. This added a level of excitement to what otherwise would have been a relatively staid afternoon culinary respite, but it also called my mind back to those words of Elliott's hymn wherein she described being "tossed about." An analogy seemed applicable to my own vocational journey, for many times I've had conflicted feelings and doubts about entering monastic life. Yet this interior tossing about is a natural part of the discernment process, and actually it may be preferable to a facile embrace of a lifestyle that requires a complete commitment.

What was it about the monks at Mirfield that compelled me to venture forth on the storm-tossed waters of the North Atlantic in order to reach them? Previously I've mentioned that I'd come to the conclusion that the Community of the Resurrection was the best match for me. The reasons for my resonance with this gathering of brethren are difficult to articulate. The Cistercian monk Michael Casey has identified the elusiveness of what draws a person to a specific community: "Often a candidate is attracted to a particular monastery without quite knowing why.... Some trivial aspect of daily life

---

[5] The New English Hymnal 294

awakens a deep inner resonance within that signals to inquirers that this is not only a place where they can seek and serve God, it is also the possibility for them to be and become themselves."[6]

On the first occasion when I'd visited Mirfield, one of the things that surprised me and created a positive impression was encountering monks who were unabashedly friendly, down-to-earth people. It was obvious that these were real people grounded in the realities of this world even though they were connecting closely and daily with things spiritual. They aspire to commune intimately with God, but their encounters with things sacred does not keep them from being able to engage with the panoply of humanity. Perhaps it was an element of the British esprit that impressed me as I experienced their courtesy coupled with a welcome? Their embrace of the traditional monastic principles of hospitality made them attentive to my needs as a guest, and the little gestures of etiquette that they practised fostered an atmosphere of generosity that reached out to embrace the strangers who visited them. Summarising my initial impressions I would say that the monks at Mirfield revealed a way of life centred upon God but tempered by humility and humour.

It was these characteristics, plus many more that I've not mentioned, that exerted an attraction for me to the monastic life of the Community of the Resurrection. In a sermon given upon the occasion of Brother Bernard's life profession at Holy Cross Monastery, Sister Hildegard Pleva said of him that he "has found that place to which he mysteriously feels that he belongs."[7] Although the specific details of what made Mirfield resonate with me are difficult to articulate, the fact is that from the outset of my first visit I felt a comforting sense of belonging. I am an American by birth, but it was within this community in England that I felt myself to be "at home." This attraction was strong enough to overcome my reservations about uprooting myself from the United States and making a transatlantic migration in order to embark upon a way of life at odds with the norms of contemporary society.

Once I had crossed the enormous oceanic expanse that the British popularly refer to as "the pond," I discovered quickly that although entering monastic life was fraught with hurdles, the far greater

---

[6] Michael Casey, Strangers to the City, p. 187.
[7] Hildegard Pleva, Mundi Medicina, Vol. XXII, No. 1, Epiphany 2010.

challenge actually was in staying! It does not take long for the magnetic appeal of the great mystery that one senses initially to morph into the dull routines and the tiresome disciplines that comprise so much of daily life in a community of religious. Eventually even the most enthusiastic entrants reach a point when the golden glow of the honeymoon is over and fidelity is sorely tested. My own commitment has been tested myriad times as life within the cloistered walls came to be viewed through the realities of untinted lenses rather than through the rose-coloured hues of my first days of blissful enchantment.

One reason that I found the adaptation to communal life a challenge was because I was not entering in the fresh bloom of youth. There is a cliché that says *"You cannot teach an old dog new tricks,"* yet here I was commencing this new venture when already firmly entrenched in my middle-aged ways. At the time of entering the Community of the Resurrection I was forty-four years old and had become used to the independent lifestyle that I'd been enjoying for the past couple of decades. This self-reliance was reinforced by the ethos of individualism that is a characteristic of American culture, so my entrance into this communal life was not easy. Monastic life is a very intense form of living that requires suppleness in relationships and this presented quite a challenge for an "old dog" like me.

Through the course of further conversations with the monks I discovered that some of them had entered when they were in their thirties or forties. Looking at these brethren, some now octogenarians, I was inspired by their examples. Their presence demonstrated that it is possible for a middle-aged person to pursue a monastic call and still be following it faithfully forty years later. As part of my programme of readings in the novitiate, I came across these words by the Cistercian monk Charles Cummings which gave me hope for a successful monastic vocation even when embarked upon in middle age.

"By the time people reach the mid-middle years, forty-five to fifty-five, they may be psychologically better prepared to settle down permanently. For several decades they have been constantly *doing* things, and now they become more appreciative of values connected with simply *being*: being themselves, being faithful, being here from now on, being fully present. As the years go on, it becomes more important to know that they belong somewhere, that they have a place where they are completely at home."[8]

That paragraph describes my personal longing to "settle down," and it was a pleasure to experience the feeling of "belonging" from the time of my earliest encounters with this monastic community. From the beginning they accepted me despite all of my personal baggage. Monks and nuns are justly famous for their hospitality, and the Benedictine rule obligates them to extend hospitality to everyone who presents themselves at the monastery, but I still was surprised that they graciously and generously embraced me with welcoming arms. I knew that I brought with me some significant baggage in the form of being a foreigner, middle-aged, previously married and divorced, and having an adult daughter. So it was with relief that I received their welcome because these aspects of my personal life and history were weighing upon me as possible barriers that I feared might prove to be insurmountable obstacles to my desired entrance into their community.

George Mikes, an author of Hungarian origin, wrote "Once a foreigner, always a foreigner. There is no way out. He may become British; he can never become English."[9] Upon one level that is reality that I've experienced when I relocated overseas and entered an Anglican religious community situated in the northern English county of West Yorkshire. No matter how long I live here, I'll never become a "local" or understand the nuances of British humour. Even if someday I should happen to acquire a British passport, there still will be the indelible imprint of my American identity which always will remain visible.

Home is not synonymous with nationality or with a specific geographical place, and it is possible for a person to find themselves in their natal land and still feel very much like a fish out of water. The gift that I experienced when entering this community was the way in which they embraced me and made me feel an essential and valued participant in their family. Undoubtedly my manner of speaking and other cultural quirks convey repeatedly my national heritage, but despite the cultural peculiarities that must have confronted them as they incorporated me into their life they have proved to be unstinting in their acceptance of me.

---

[8] Charles Cummings, Monastic Practices, p. 165.
[9] George Mikes, How To Be An Alien, p. 12.

I came into the monastery carrying with me some significant emotional and relational burdens, and the brokenness of my domestic life was evidenced by my seeking to become a monk whilst also having an ex-wife and a daughter. Throughout my life I have agonised over my personal failures and berated myself for the myriad shortcomings that were mine in the marital, parental or familial realms. Reading the gospels is a restorative remedy for me because they demonstrate that Jesus did not find our sins to be terribly worrisome or insurmountable problems. Jesus freely and unhesitatingly forgave sins and it seemed to be a relatively simple action that the Lord was happy to do. In St. Matthew's gospel, Christ says *"Take heart, my son; your sins are forgiven."*[10] Similarly, in St. Luke's gospel Jesus says *"Your sins are forgiven...your faith has saved you, go in peace."*[11] The Saviour didn't feel a need to distance himself from the taint of proximity to sinful humanity, and he did not hold himself aloof from fallen folk no matter what their reputation. In Christ's actions I have found hope, especially in those times when I've berated myself for my faults and failures.

To my gladness this same Christ-like nature was manifest within the Community of the Resurrection as they reached out to welcome me. I remain thankful for their willingness in having accepted me even though the track record of my personal life showed sad occasions of failure. Shortly before I moved to England I'd written a letter to my friends in which I'd conveyed the news about the anticipated migration into monastic life that I was planning. In that letter I expressed how much I was looking forward to entering into a community that had demonstrated the warmth of unconditional acceptance upon my previous visits. I also acknowledged that lately I had been shifting locations annually in interim ministry, and thus I was looking forward to the stability of being rooted within a permanent community. Addressing this theme of stability in my letter I wrote this:

> "Since the end of the 19th century the Anglican monks of the Community of the Resurrection have been residing on the very same site in the Yorkshire town of Mirfield, so it will be a great blessing for me to enter into the historical continuity and stability that they offer after I've spent so many semi-

---

[10] Matthew 9:2
[11] Luke 7:48 & 50

16

nomadic years engaged in various missionary and interim ministries."[12]

Not all visitors who call on the monks at Mirfield find themselves attracted to this community. Some people regard us and our customs as a bit archaic. But I believe that the timelessness that characterises monks and nuns is due to the intentional embrace of a lifestyle different from that of society outside of the monastic enclosure. This life embodies Christian values that are fundamentally different from popular culture. Yet this is not an attachment to a romanticised past, and they are forward looking in desiring to serve the contemporary Church. This ongoing engagement with society was impressed upon me when, a couple of weeks after my arrival, Archbishop Desmond Tutu came and blessed the foundation stone intended for our planned eco-friendly monastery. Even a century-long history of being lodged at the House of the Resurrection is not preventing them from looking ahead and moving forward in response to the dynamic prodding of the Holy Spirit.

The buildings presently occupied by the Community of the Resurrection may be historically interesting but they are cold and draughty and logistically impractical for monastic life. Fortunately the primary attraction for me was the welcoming spirit of the brethren who made me feel at home in this environment. The home which I've found is not a geographical place or a specific pile of bricks and stone. Instead it is the community of these persons who share a mutual commitment to God and to one another. That provides the sense of this being my spiritual abode. Father Huntington, founder of the Order of the Holy Cross, wrote in his Rule this comment about a monastery: "It is our home for a time, but it is so only because the house and all that is in it belong to God and we belong to him. It is a house that God has claimed for himself."[13] My call to the religious life involved feeling drawn to this particular group of men who are visibly the Body of Christ. Some of them are peculiar individuals, but even after living amongst them for several years I can say with confidence that these are holy men whose lives reveal to me glimpses of God. Through my participation in the monastic life I am journeying into deeper intimacy

---

[12] Letter of Dennis B. A. Berk, *unpublished,* September 2009.
[13] Rule of James Huntington and his Successors, p. 31.

with Jesus, and this is made possible through my daily interactions with the brethren in this community.

Chapter 3 : Genuine Satisfaction Guaranteed

Glimpses of God are revealed to me through my monastic brothers with whom I am living. Sometimes these revelations of God are manifest in surprising ways and through personal channels that I've regarded as rather unlikely conveyors of divine grace. This happens because God is reaching out to all of humankind constantly and perpetually. Humans are made in the image of God, and thus we contain an imprint of some of the divine attributes. Given the nature of our inheritance from the Great Creator in whose image we have been fashioned, it is natural that one of our fundamental desires is for transcendence. Although it is difficult to define what we want to attain in the pursuit of this lofty goal, none the less even in our confused muddle we continue to aspire towards transcendence. Some of the ways in which I've sought out elements of this have been through the sacrament of marriage, through the conception and birth of a child, and through the publication of books as a literary legacy. Time has proven to me that many of the avenues upon which I've travelled in an effort to connect with something bigger than my own finite self have turned out to be incomplete means by which to satisfy my heart's innermost longings.

Since life is a gift given by God it seems natural to want to respond by offering oneself back to the God from whom all blessings originally came in the first place. Upon entering this Community I did not have a clear idea of how to achieve that offering of myself for God's service within a monastic setting. Speaking of his own journey, the Benedictine monk Mark Barrett has written in words that echo my own sentiment: "I began my life as a monk with the conviction that, if I threw myself into it with sufficient vigour, the tradition passed down through the centuries would, as if by magic, provide me with the answers I was seeking to all of life's dilemmas."[14] Like Barrett, soon after my entrance into monastic life I discovered that monasticism does not provide facile answers.

Despite monasticism's centuries of tradition, and a membership composed of committed Christians in which there are many saintly souls, the hallowed places within the cloistered world cannot deliver a magical formula that instantaneously enlightens and elevates new entrants to levels of intimate communion with God. I am not denying

---

[14] Mark Barrett, Crossing, p. 4.

the efficacy of monastic life by saying that joining a religious community will not automatically bestow a deluge of spiritual riches without the individual making any effort. The desire for God that propels one to commence a monastic journey may indeed come to fruition, but the rigours of the daily walk of faith cannot be avoided. The pilgrimage that every Christian is called to make simply must be done because it is within the process of journeying that the spiritual fruit ripens to maturity.

The prophet Jeremiah records God as saying: "When you call upon me and come and pray to me, I will hear you. When you search for me, you will find me if you seek me with all your heart."[15] Earnestly seeking to serve God, I arrived at the House of the Resurrection as part of my search. Misguided though I was when making my initial approach, yet my intentions were sincere because my fervent desire was to commune frequently and deeply with God. Our spiritual desires do not exist within a separate compartment of life, so it is impossible to draw a boundary between the material and the spiritual realms. The bottom line is that the whole of human life is innately spiritual. Our desires are not irreconcilable with spiritual growth because almost every kind of desire holds within it the possibility of being touched and transformed by the Holy Spirit.

Saint Catherine of Siena, a fourteenth-century Italian nun and mystic, recognised the extraordinary power of our desires when she wrote about how they are one of the few ways that humans have of touching God because we have nothing infinite except our soul's love and desire.[16] Not all desires that we experience are beneficial or healthy, and some desires may enslave us or lead to the dissipation of our energies. Not everything ought to be satisfied merely because we want it. However, righteous desires can generate emotional power and physical energy with the resulting enrichment and strengthening of our spirituality. Thus the pursuit of their satisfaction is commendable.

If a particular desire is right and proper, and if it is pursued with prayerful discernment, then God will bring that desire to fruition. It will become an irresistible longing burning away within us and inspiring us with a passion to live into that desire which God has planted inside us. From the time of my first introduction to the

---

[15] Jeremiah 29:12-13
[16] Catherine of Siena, Dialogue, p. 270.

Community of the Resurrection, and throughout the subsequent years, the intensity of the fire that is the vocational call kept increasing until it reached the point where it seemed obvious that this was where I wanted to be *and* where God wanted me to be.

Prior Bede, of Holy Cross Monastery in New York, said in his blog: "We want a man to be able to say: 'Yes, I really want this. I really do.' And we trust that God wants it as well, and our discernment process will include, as his training goes on, a continued search for the ways in which our will and God's will intervene."[17] When I made the decision committing me to packing up my life and relocating overseas to join a community living together under religious vows, I was saying to myself "Yes, I really do want to be a monk!" By no means did that simple statement result in my automatic attainment of such a vocation. All that I was doing in that initial step was proclaiming aloud my desire. Then I had to embark upon the pursuit of it and fervently trust in God to bring it to fruition.

> "To desire heaven is to want God and to love Him with a love the monks sometimes call impatient. The greater desire becomes, the more the soul rests in God. Possession increases in the same proportion as desire. But just as death is the condition upon which full satisfaction depends, so this pre-taste demands that we must die to the world... This obligation is incumbent upon all Christians, all the faithful are called upon to detach themselves from the world and to cling to God...."[18]

Those words were written by the Benedictine monk Jean Leclercq, and my personal experience similarly has been one of growing in desire for this particular expression of the Christian vocation. This happens in conjunction with the increase in my willingness to rest entirely in God and offer myself to his service. Since the autumn of 2009 when I ventured "across the pond" to test the waters of a monastic vocation, I've discovered that the more I open up myself to God then the more my desire for intimate communion with God blossoms. This desire is not something that is limited to nuns and monks. It is not the exclusive possession of people wearing clerical collars or dressed in monastic habits. Instead it is something incumbent

---

[17] Bede Mudge, Mundi Medicina, Eastertide 2009, p. 1.
[18] Jean Leclercq, Love of Learning and Desire for God, p. 86.

21

upon all Christians. Whether or not residing inside or outside of a cloister's walls, we ought to strive to detach ourselves from overdependence upon the world and should cling to God who alone can satisfy our desire. Only within God can we find the genuine satisfaction of our soul's deepest longing, and it is guaranteed that God can indeed fully satisfy us!

Chapter 4: Schedules – Mine or Thine?

I recall vividly my arrival at the House of the Resurrection on the evening of 22nd October 2009. It had been a long ordeal of travelling that commenced with an international flight whose destination was Gatwick airport near London. Then a domestic flight shuttled me to Manchester's airport, where I boarded a train that conveyed me to Huddersfield and then I switched to a bus that took me to Mirfield. Exhausted from the journey, I summoned up energy to overcome my fatigue and staggered wearily through the monastery's gates hauling my heavy suitcases behind me.

In that moment of entering I was aware of leaving behind much of what had become second nature to me after more than four decades of living in the secular world. The magnitude of this new venture weighed upon me even more heavily than my fully-packed suitcases as I realised that now I had taken a major step upon a vocational journey whose future I was unable to predict. Even the present situation seemed largely beyond my control, for on admission I was entrusting myself to a programme that would be directed by a Novice Guardian into whose hands I was placing myself on this journey of discernment.

The town to which I'd arrived is situated in a region known as Calderdale – one of many dales found within this area of northern England. Mirfield is located in the West Riding of Yorkshire, where it perches upon the hillsides and nestles in a valley formed by the River Calder. Lying within the heart of what once was a famous woollens district, its smoke-grimed buildings still recall its previous industrial heritage. Here in this Yorkshire town is located an Anglican brotherhood known as the Community of the Resurrection. The main building in which they live is a nineteenth century mansion, and it does not actually bear the formal title of a monastery or an abbey. Instead, inscribed in Latin above the front door, are these words: *Domus Resurrectionis*. So it is simply a house dedicated to the resurrection of our Lord Jesus Christ. This house, augmented by an unwieldy hodgepodge of later additions, has been described as a residence recalling "the times when mill owners made money rapidly and took steps to impress the fact on the outside world."[19] However this house is overshadowed by the Community's church that towers over every other building and dominates the entire site. Although now drastically

---

[19] Peter Anson, Call of the Cloister, p. 123.

23

altered by a recent renovation, as it was constructed originally the historian Peter Anson said of this church building:

> "It is original in design and no other church in England resembles it. The architect, the late Sir Walter Tapper, derived his inspiration both from Byzantine and Romanesque styles. The predominant note of the interior is one of extreme simplicity. The cream walls of the nave intensify the rich red of the sandstone columns and arches surrounding the sanctuary."[20]

That church building, with its soaring arches conveying a powerful sense of the transcendence of God, draws people to the deeply mysterious Divine that is greater than themselves. If they are like me then those who enter also are longing for an encounter with the Word made flesh. For that intimacy to be experienced the love of God must be incarnated through those whom one is meeting.

From the occasion of my first contact with the Community of the Resurrection I had a profound sense of how the brethren were incarnating the love of God in their welcome. Immediately after my arrival I was shown to the room in which I would lodge. In traditional monastic parlance this room is called a "cell," but that term seldom is used here. Upon walking into that room for the first time I was struck by its smallness and austerity. The starkness of its white walls, the sparse furniture, and the lack of plush fabrics in coordinated designs instantly gave me an impression of asceticism in keeping with the image that comes to people's minds when they envision the abode of a monk or a nun. Possibly a fleeting glimpse of something less than enthusiasm was revealed upon my face because the Novice Guardian smiled reassuringly at me and said, "This isn't to be your nest. The whole monastery is your home." Since my assigned room in the monastery was not even as big as the smallest of the four bedrooms in my former residence, I found comfort in being told that this one room which I'd entered did not constitute the entirety of my domestic domain. In keeping with its original nineteenth-century erection as a manor house fit for a wealthy woollen magnate, this building has some lovely spaces within it. In no time at all I'd settled in and was finding myself at home in this environment.

---

[20] Ibid.

No sooner had I begun to get acclimatised than I discovered that I would have to depart from England due to some documentation complications. A newly instituted points-based immigration system was adversely affecting the length of my initial stay, and I was required to exit the United Kingdom in order to apply for an extended-stay visa from within my country of origin. Less than two months after my arrival I returned to the airport in Manchester and boarded a flight to travel back across the Atlantic Ocean to Pennsylvania.

When I first received the news that I had to leave the U.K. much earlier than I'd anticipated, I argued with God in an effort to evoke some sort of divine intervention that would spare me from this unwanted transatlantic trip. In my prayers I told God that making another international journey so soon after my previous one would be poor financial stewardship. With seemingly sound reasoning I explained to God the folly of wasting money on another set of airline tickets. Surely those funds could be better used in God's service instead of going into the pockets of an airline?

God was intent upon showing me that my spiritual maturation was of far more value than the money that I wanted to avoid spending on airfare. I should have known to trust God's stewardship, after all God does not waste anything. Everything in our lives happens for a reason and a major part of that reason is to help us grow in faith. I've heard it said that life is lived in a forward motion but that it only can be understood by looking back. This calls for our trusting in the loving purposes of God. Perhaps the biggest challenge is believing that God is in control when life seems to be quite out of control.

One gift that resulted from my return to the United States was the opportunity to celebrate the Christmas season of 2009 with my parents, my daughter, my sister and her family. However once the new year arrived then my frustration began to increase as, with growing anxiousness, I continued to await word about the status of my immigration application. Saint James, in the first chapter of his epistle, says "whenever you face trials of any kind, consider it nothing but joy, because you know that the testing of your faith produces patience."[21]

Despite those edifying words I definitely was not feeling patient. My patience was running out as one month of waiting followed another one. Back in November the Community of the Resurrection had

---

[21] James 1:2-3

submitted their application to sponsor me, but no signs were visible upon the horizon showing significant progress being made. Time kept passing but I did not seem to be getting any closer to being in possession of the essential paperwork that would grant me long-term residence upon the soil of 'merrie olde England.'

As I spent my time at Holy Cross Monastery's location alongside the Hudson River in New York, I tried to puzzle out what God's purpose might be for me. What was God trying to achieve by permitting my much-desired monastic journey to be aborted so soon after its commencement? I wanted to offer myself to God, so why didn't the Almighty sort out my immigration paperwork to facilitate a monastic vocation?

Upon further reflection I realised that I'd expected to offer God the gift of myself in *my* time, according to *my* schedule, and within the plan that *I* had arranged many months in advance. Since monasteries are not swamped beneath a flood of aspirants seeking admission, I'd reasoned that God ought to be grateful for my willingness to leave "the world" and embrace such a lifestyle. But a couple months of prayerful discernment spent with the monks of Holy Cross enabled me to see how egocentric the imposition of my own timeline was upon this call that God was testing within me.

I embarked upon the pursuit of a monastic vocation with the expectation that it would come to fruition in the exact moment that would be most convenient for me. One of Satan's temptations is for us to seize hold of something and grasp it as our "right" instead of receiving it as God's gift. This is an age-old problem for humanity. In the garden of Eden, when Satan approached Adam and Eve, they were tempted with the offer of being able to attain all the gifts of God at that moment in which they desired to have them. According to the silken words of the serpent they would not have to wait patiently because they could partake of the instant gratification promised by the tantalizingly forbidden fruit. Thus they experienced the forfeiture of abundant life on God's terms. Unfortunately it seems that I have not evolved very far from my biblical ancestors, for I still desired the immediate gratification of my vocational desires.

After this recognition of the impetuous nature of my vocational strivings had penetrated my mind, I was able to step back from trying to order God's arrangements for my life. This helped me to rest more contentedly in the time of waiting that was allotted to me. Finally an envelope arrived from the British Consulate in Los Angeles, inside which was the necessary documentation granting me permission to return to the U.K. and reside there for an extended stay.

I recall the feeling of elation experienced when receiving the news of my visa's approval. Apparently my exuberance was noticeable to the other brethren of Holy Cross, because that morning as I sat inside their monastery's Chapter Room the Superior looked at me and commented that I was glowing. This might not have been due entirely to the recent buoyancy of my emotional state. Perhaps it was a result of the sunshine cascading in through the stained glass windows and casting a beam of coloured light upon me as I sat in my chair? But part of my glow was from the smile etched upon my face ever since I'd received the affirmative news from the British Consulate.

After more than three months spent residing outside of England I was eager to "return home," and that was the sensation that I experienced when I entered the House of the Resurrection after my absence. As I walked through those doors I felt the comforting sense of knowing that I was in a place where I really belonged. This was a community that had become another family for me, and I was excited to be back amongst my brothers-in-Christ with whom I could continue to learn how to live and love more like Jesus.

Not long after my return the time came for me to take a further step deeper into their communal life. After months spent as a postulant "testing the waters" of monasticism, I was deemed ready for admission as a novice. A "novice" is defined as "a member of a community who is in the formation stage of the Religious Life, when she or he learns the mind, work and spirit of the particular community whilst living amongst the members."[22] I'd already been in the initial formation stage for some months, but the spiritual walk through this earthly life entails always being engaged in ongoing formation. My admission to the novitiate actually was a formal recognition of my continuation in the monastic journey that I'd commenced the previous autumn.

A person becomes a novice in a ceremony commonly known as "the clothing," wherein one receives the "habit" that is the distinctive apparel of the religious community that they are joining. For me this entailed donning a grey scapular atop my black cassock and receiving a brass cross to hang from my belt. The monastic habit, of whatever

---

[22] Anglican Religious Life, p. 189.

style it may be, is a symbol proclaiming that the person wearing such garb is striving to take Christianity *very* seriously by seeking to realise within their life the full counsels of the Saviour. In this way every monk and nun is a powerful visual sign of a deep and all-consuming commitment to Jesus Christ.

The Cistercian monk Adalbert de Vogue asserts that nuns and monks being "set apart and made conspicuous by their habit, will feel more obliged to act as they should.... It will constantly remind them, as well as those who see them, of their resolution to lead a perfect life, of which it is a sign." The wearing of a garment that is distinctively counter-cultural to the contemporary trends of secular fashion makes nuns and monks conspicuous, and sometimes I've found that the attention this unique garb draws from onlookers has resulted in my feeling awkwardly self-conscious. At such times I've wished that I was wearing something less conspicuous, but de Vogue's asserts that "we should have the courage to wear it everywhere, outside as well as at home, for nothing is more degrading for a monk than to act our religious folklore behind the cloister and to camouflage himself as a secular when he goes out."[23]

The occasion of my official "clothing" in this conspicuous garment took place at the celebration of the first Solemn Evensong of Pentecost, and I looked forward eagerly to the arrival of that great feast day. When the 22nd May arrived it seemed that God's schedule had caught up with my own desires. Finally the monastic vocation to which I had aspired for some time was coming into my grasp. Even though I was on the verge of taking another step further into the religious life, I had not developed a mature perspective upon it. I still was viewing this journey from an individualistic vantage point as I endeavoured to wrap God into conformity with my plans. My outward vesture was not the primary thing that needed to be changed and clothed in something new. More importantly I needed to have my inner attitude transformed so that I would cease telling God what I wanted and begin discerning what God wanted from me.

The Eve of Pentecost arrived, and as the evening sunlight filtered in through the windows of the chapel I took my position in front of the altar and knelt before the Superior for the ceremony of my formal admission as a novice. That was the moment when I was vested in the

---

[23] Adalbert de Vogue, Rule of St. Benedict: A Doctrinal, pp. 272 & 278.

habit that is distinctive to this Community, but since then I've come to realise that the outward apparel received that evening only serves as a symbol. This insight was illuminated for me the next morning when, in the festal Mass celebrated on the Day of Pentecost, I heard with newly opened ears the lyrics of the third verse of Bianco da Siena's 15th century hymn "Come down, O love divine" which says: "Let holy charity mine outward vesture be, and lowliness become mine inner clothing."[24] The monastic attire in which I was newly clad would bring no enhancement to my spiritual maturity unless accompanied by the inner graces of Christian love and compassionate service. I appreciate the symbolism of the habit, and value its identification of me as a member of the Community of the Resurrection, but this vesture is secondary in importance to the inner clothing of the Spirit that must clothe the entirety of my being.

---

[24] Bianco da Siena, *Come Down, O Love Divine*, New English Hymnal 137

Chapter 5: Adept at Adapting?

Now that I was a novice, dressed in garb that clearly associated me with the Community of the Resurrection, I began to participate more in the activities involved in the daily life of a monastery. Many aspects of the novitiate programme were not easy for me. Forty-four years old at the time of joining, I was accustomed to an independent lifestyle marked by the individualism and self-sufficiency of American culture. Being middle-aged my flexibility was not what it once was, and this fact became increasingly obvious whenever I found myself lacking the necessary suppleness in relationships that is essential for harmony within this intense form of community living. I asked myself, "Am I adept enough to adapt to this communal life that I've entered?"

Peter Levi, a professor at Oxford who'd been a Jesuit for twenty-eight years, has said of the novitiate that it "is a time when not so much the genuineness as the durability of a religious vocation is tested. A temporary enthusiasm can be genuine enough, but religious institutions insist on permanence and stability."[25] With excitement I'd embraced everything monastic at the commencement of my journey, but as time moved on and my emotional high wore down then the stamina required for navigating successfully through the novitiate became readily apparent. Previously my eyes had been clouded by the golden glow of the "honeymoon" in which I'd found myself at the onset of my vocational journey, but now the intensity involved in absorbing a new lifestyle was impacting me personally.

I desired to commune with God, but the demanding rhythm of activities that characterises monastic life kept impinging upon my daily schedule. Having my entire routine mapped out for me, needing to ask permissions from my guardians, living under the constant evaluative gaze of the brethren, and being at the beck and call of them grated against my penchant for being in control of my own life. After having been the "head honcho" in parishes where I'd exercised a considerable amount of authority, it was a shock to be stripped of responsibility and power. No longer was I the rector whose clerical position authorised me to make decisions and delegate tasks to other people. The props that previously had given me status now were removed, and as a chronologically mature novice I found it challenging to adapt to this new situation.

---

[25] Peter Levi, Frontiers of Paradise, p. 202.

A member of the Order of the Holy Cross, commenting upon his experiences as a novice, expressed thoughts congruent with my own feelings: "Spiritual formation in monastic life lays open your life and soul before God and begins a process of divine therapy. So much of this process affects one psychologically and emotionally because that is where we do the real work of spiritual growth and change."[26] I resonated with his words because I found the novitiate challenging every fibre of my being as I struggled to open myself to the changes occurring within me on a breadth and with an intensity that I'd not anticipated. Perhaps those four decades of life prior to my arrival brought some additional rigidity resistant to this transformative process, but I continue to live in the hope that God shall bring to birth within me a new spiritual maturity.

I came with good intentions, wanting earnestly to do something noble for God through the offering of myself in vowed service to Christ. However what I'm discovering is that God is transforming me by changing my original good intentions into desires that are more in conformity with the divine will. I arrived here wanting to "do something" for God, and I harboured an expectation that I would undertake something significant as an expression of these noble spiritual endeavours to which I aspired. But I've ended up realising that the actual tasks that I'm doing are not of ultimate importance. Instead what really matters is that God is doing something to me! Previously I had that formula backwards. I'd started the equation with myself and eventually got around to involving God, but the proper way is to begin with God. Only then will everything else fall into its correct position.

Some verses upon which I've reflected during my novitiate come from Ecclesiasticus: "My child, when you come to serve the Lord, prepare yourself for testing. Set your heart right and be steadfast, and do not be impetuous in time of calamity. Cling to him and do not depart."[27] With a determination driven by a pursuit of the vocational goals to which I aspired, I entered with a single-mindedness that occasionally resulted in my lack of appreciation for the alternative pathways to which God was directing me. Too often I've been so intent upon pursuing my self-designed aspirations that I've failed to

---

[26] Charles Mizelle, Mundi Medicina, Michaelmas 2009, p. 14.
[27] Ecclesiasticus 2:1-3

discern the ways in which God is leading me into more profitable routes. At such times, when I've found myself crashing in emotional disillusionment brought about through my own stubborn wilfulness, those words from Ecclesiasticus have encouraged me to remain steadfast and reminded me to cling to God in whom is the strengthening resolve empowering me to persevere in my walk upon this spiritual pilgrimage.

Times of testing are not experienced only by novices within religious communities. Every Christian encounters occasions that test their faith. If we relied exclusively upon our own resources then none of us would have the strength to overcome that which tries our souls and tests our spirits. Retreating into an abbey or a convent is not an avenue for escape from life's challenges. Living within cloistered confines does not provide a refuge from the trials that assault one upon a daily basis. No matter where we live we cannot trust in our own resources. Our personal "baggage" follows us into a monastery when we enter. Residence inside this sheltering space does not guarantee safety or the release from our burdens. It is only within the context of our intimate communion with God that there is the hope of spiritual victory.

Prior to my entrance into monastic life for two decades I had been exercising my vocation as a priest. In that capacity I'd participated in parish ministry as a rector, and the novitiate confronted me with new customs that were contrary to some of the practices that had become ingrained within me over the course of twenty years in holy orders. Having arrived in England from the fast-paced environment of the suburban setting in which I'd been engaged in parish ministry, the markedly slower pace of monastic life caught me off guard. In the parish it was regarded as commendable to be observed rushing around busily engaged in active ministry, and members of my congregation seemed pleased to see their priest hard at work. In contrast here at the House of the Resurrection the monastic demeanour is meant to be expressed through a manner of conduct characterised by a certain *"gravitas"* conveying calmness and serenity at all times regardless of whatever circumstances are occurring.

I've consciously had to apply myself to practising what is termed as "custody of the eyes." Previously I'd found that parishioners valued my having direct eye contact with them and wanted that kind of forthright interaction. But now whenever I am in the Community's church I have to remind myself to keep my eyes demurely lowered. Not every guest who comes here is comfortable with the directness of visual contact that is typical of the candour prevalent in the American personality, so my eyes are lowered in order to give each guest their own space in which they can feel safe when they join us in worship.

Even more difficult for me to achieve than the "custody of the eyes" has been the moderation of my manner of walking. Endowed with long legs that bring my height to 6 feet, I possess a length of stride that affords an unmistakable quickness to my gait. So it takes a deliberate effort on my part to slow down my normal brisk pace to a more dignified speed. Both my vigorous walking speed and my manner of making eye contact needed adaptation to conform to the expectations of this new environment in which I am living. The normative patterns by which previously I'd conducted myself are not in keeping with the monastic demeanour. Sometimes it has been a struggle for me to remain mindful of these new behaviours, but I realise that there is genuine merit in these customs. Slowly I have come to understand that the modification of these outward behaviours actually bear fruit by enabling an inner transformation to take place within me.

My integration into the Community of the Resurrection is a two-way process, involving a mutuality of interaction, confrontation, and adaptation not only on my part but also by every other brother and is confronted by my idiosyncrasies. This integration cannot be rushed to a premature fruition. It takes place throughout each day within the context of life's experiences. Gradually, over the course of time, I am becoming more thoroughly woven into the fabric of our communal life.

The process of acculturation to monastic life is challenging because it is continuous. Life is not static and periodically new customs arise or revised policies are implemented. Even within the cloister, where many timeless traditions are treasured, life is in a constant state of change. Sometimes these are big, dramatic changes, but more often they are small and barely detectable. Both the big and the small revisions require flexibility for adaptation. Esther de Waal has written: "Hard things have to be faced. Nor is it a once-and-for-all battle; the briars grow again each year; I clear an open space, a breathing space, but it has to be reclaimed time after time."[28] As time goes on I am

---

[28] Esther de Waal, Celtic Way of Prayer, p. 104.

discovering that a monastic vocation cannot be forced. My own determination and willpower are not enough.

Fortunately I do not have to rely upon my own strength. This is a great relief because alone I do not possess adequate resources to achieve the transformative goal of becoming more Christ-like in every aspect and dimension of life. I am accompanied on this spiritual journey by my monastic brothers. Even more importantly I have the assurance of knowing that I am always in the loving company of God. Therein is the strengthening support that makes all things possible.

Chapter 6: Migratory Patterns

Mobility is a characteristic of modern life, and in the 21st century people frequently move around and shift from one place to another. Not only does our place of residence change, but so too does our work, our relationships, and our commitments. We seem to be constantly in motion, and I confess to fitting into this lifestyle pattern. Like many others of my generation, I had a hunger for personal contact yet I was fearful of making a commitment. I felt a need for permanence and stability but was living a life of continual disruptions amidst frequently shifting locations. Looking back through the lens of hindsight I am able to see the considerable migratory history of my own past.

My mother hails from Michigan while my father was born in Pennsylvania. My parents met in Ohio, when they were students at Malone College, and that mid-western state is the same one in which I was born. When I was a toddler we moved to Pennsylvania and there I spent my childhood years. Upon graduating from high school I went to Illinois to pursue an undergraduate degree in psychology at Wheaton College. Then I crossed an international border to study theology at Trinity College in Toronto. During those years at seminary I met a Canadian woman who was to become my wife after graduation. There in the Canadian province of Ontario I was ordained, we married, had a daughter, and I served as a parish priest. Upon the dissolution of my marriage I returned to Pennsylvania and pursued a doctorate, followed by some post-graduate studies at Oxford in England.

Later I broadened my horizons further as a lecturer at a theological college in the African nation of Zambia. Within the relatively moderate span of my life I have exercised my priestly ministry upon three continents: having served in Canada, the United States, England and Zambia. One result of these continual migrations has been the modulation of my speech as, unconsciously, I've picked up bits of dialectal inflection from each of the areas in which I've resided. The result is that I no longer sound distinctly like any one nationality. To this day people meeting me for the first time have difficulty identifying my national origins due to the hodgepodge of linguistic patterns that now have become a natural part of my speech.

Although that may sound like an unusual migratory journey, I've discovered that a considerable number of my peers have an equally lengthy list of places in which they've resided. Schools, jobs and homes now are changed almost as casually as we change our clothes. Nearly everything in contemporary life is immediate and fluid in this mobile Western world. Wireless technology is able to move with us as we travel from one place to another. The result is that our lives have become so mobile that we are losing a sense of rootedness. In our quest for freedom we are falling into the trap of selfishness and its accompanying loneliness, and these are becoming endemic in our culture. As we become absorbed in amusing ourselves in an effort to attain personal satisfaction, we are failing to make deep connections with those who are around us.

Recognising this pattern of aimlessness in my shifting from one locale to another, by the time of my fortieth birthday I was at a stage in life where I desired to plant some roots that would ground me solidly to something. Initially I'd thought that this quest for permanent roots would direct me to a specific place of residence, but I've discovered that monastic stability is not based upon being tied to one geographic site. It is established on being rooted in the unchanging fidelity of God. The essence of the monastic framework is not lodged in a place, rather it is found in Someone. First and foremost this is the Divine One whom we worship as the Triune God, but upon a secondary level it also is manifest through the people with whom we live.

There are some fundamentals that are common to the monastic life, of which such things as the liturgy, contemplation and meditation, study, and manual labour are but a few on what is a lengthy list. Within those activities I encounter face to face my monastic brothers. Each of them has been chosen by God to be here – which is the only way that this assemblage of individuals could have occurred. If the selection of them had been left in my hands then there are some whom I would not have chosen to live with, and no doubt it is equally true that some of them might not have wanted to live with me! Thankfully God's wisdom surpasses my own, and we've been brought together into a spiritual family through our shared kinship with the heavenly Father.

Together we are travelling on a spiritual journey that is much greater in its challenges than I'd bargained for upon my entrance. Fortunately it also is much more rewarding that anything that I could have imagined. This 'family in Christ' that I've joined sometimes is experienced as a blessing which evokes heartfelt appreciation and gratitude, but at other times it can be a bane that I endure with irritable grumbling under my breath. However at the end of each day I realise that it is this combination of highs and lows encountered in the course of interacting with my monastic brothers that is producing within me a greater personal maturity. "The vow of stability commits a monk or nun to live with the same group of people for life. Finding the right monastery is about finding a community where you feel at home, where you can grow spiritually and as a person despite, or even on account of, the inevitable up and down of any living relationship."[29] Stability means that I commit myself to embracing this community as it is and not merely the ideal of what I want it to be.

After several decades spent shifting from one place to another the vow of stability exerted a strong appeal to me. Almost from the beginning of my first visit I sensed a mysterious 'at-homeness' as my heart resonated with the Community of the Resurrection. I had reached a stage in life where I no longer desired to keep wandering to various parts of the globe. Here I've discovered an interior dimension of stability that is characterised by a profound contentment. Yet I also realise that this sense of being 'at-home' in Mirfield cannot be based only upon this geographical locale. As I was packing up my belongings in the rectory, the awareness of Christians being a 'pilgrim people' struck me anew when I received an email from the Superior about plans for a new monastery. At the same time that I was preparing to relocate from Pennsylvania to England, the brethren of the Community were studying architectural plans portraying the new residence into which they hope to relocate.

My commitment must be one of fidelity to the journey itself, and this entails a willingness to travel upon routes that are changing and not fixed rigidly in place. Stability asserts that I am walking on the road of life to its end with these people who now have become my family-in-Christ, and I must continue this journey with them no matter how the circumstances may change. The sanctification of relationships, and the discovery of friendships within the diversity of contrasting personalities, are part and parcel of the embrace of stability. This is true of Christian life both inside and outside of monastic confines.

The call of Jesus that invites us to the abundant life is an invitation for *every* Christian to live deeply in all of their relationships. It is neither beneficial nor satisfying for us to flit from one person to another, from one place to another, and from one job to another as

---

[29] Laurentia Johns, editor, Touched by God, p. 86.

commonly is done these days. In stark contrast to this 21st century lifestyle, most of our ancestors stayed at one job for a lifetime just as they probably lived in their hometown all of their lives. Continual choices and constant changes were not a luxury that they had available to select, so it could be said that stability was the natural default pattern that characterised their existence.

With the increase in potential pathways that are open to our pursuit in today's world, it is easy to be overwhelmed by the myriad options and to lose our way within a maze of convoluted avenues that prove to be diversions leading only to dead ends. How quickly so many of those initially appealing routes wind up leading to superficial rewards whose fleeting nature leaves us disappointed and depressed. Contemporary life, with its array of attractive choices, is not an easy journey to navigate successfully. None the less it's a journey that we all must make. When strengthened and sustained by Christ who accompanies us then we can reach the ultimate destination.

Inevitably there will be failures and successes, triumphs and tragedies, within the profound risks that we take in life and love. No one except the incarnate Son of God ever managed to traverse this earthly journey without succumbing to sin. Admittedly such a sad track record has been the case for me within a variety of domestic and vocational forums. Although painful when I experienced them at the time, those occasions of failure have proven to be learning opportunities that moved me beyond the façade of self that I preferred to project to observers. Like a butterfly engaged in the arduous task of emerging from its cocoon, those situations were a struggle for me. But they've also moved me to an acceptance and embrace of my real self that would not have happened if I'd remained like a caterpillar comfortably reposing within its cocoon. Through those experiences I have come to realise the importance of refraining from packing up my suitcases and running away from difficulties confronting me. The grass is not greener on the other side of the fence. Even if you flee there, within almost no time at all you'll discover that the same weeds also grow just as tenaciously on your new side of the fence as they did in that place you'd so recently vacated.

Reflecting upon the ancient monastic tradition of stability, I believe that it implies a commitment to stay engaged in the work of slogging through a lifelong discernment process pursued in the quest for understanding oneself, others, and God. This is expressed by an attitude of determination to remain within the monastic community that has become one's adoptive family. At the core of this traditional monastic virtue is the quality of permanence: not leaving when the voyage on the seas of life gets rough. Some monastic communities inhabit ancient buildings in which they have dwelt for centuries, but the permanence to which nuns and monks are committed is not to an actual building. A particular building may be cherished for a variety of reasons, some of them nostalgic and sentimental, but the essence of the religious life is not in the bricks and mortar no matter how aesthetically attractive that masonry may be. As the monk Michael Casey says, "Stability is not immobility. It is the knack of remaining constant in the midst of change."[30]

The vow of stability in the Benedictine tradition is not intended to attach a person to a specific set of buildings. There is no inherent virtue in being locked into a particular pile of wood, bricks, stone or anything else. Stability is meant to connect a person to a group of people. The full realisation of the vow of stability is a life enterprise that is taken together in companionship with fellow travellers. As such I've come to understand that I am responsible for the others in my life not only when it is convenient to be engaged with them. The reality is that I am responsible every day for each one of these persons to whom I am relating. Furthermore I shall continue to be responsible to them, and they to me, until we have helped each other all the way through this earthly journey.

Living in the same place with the same people twenty-four hours a day and seven days as week is a daunting challenge. Sometimes I am not confident that I'm adequately equipped for this sort of life. Perhaps due to the legacy of time spent in some exotic parts of this world, one of the hardest things has been staying put and letting the monastic process run its course at its own pace. Stability is teaching me that no matter what difficulties surround me, if I stay rooted in my relationships with my brothers then eventually I will find God present right here in our midst.

Mobility tempts me from this interior stillness. Many allures attract me to the grass which always seems to be greener anywhere else than here. Images conveyed by society can be an enticing lure drawing me away from the commitments that I ought to honour. The appealing

---

[30] Michael Casey, Strangers to the City, p. 191.

displays and posters in shop windows hold out the promise of greater satisfaction than is offered by our present state of discontent. "Buy this product and life will be better" or "Travel to tropical 'N' and you'll be happy" are what their advertisements proclaim in vivid colours. Similarly other relationships can tempt me with the promises of a more rewarding and pleasurable partnership.

Every new place and new person could entice me to leave this monastery in order to pursue elsewhere that elusive hunt for others more perfectly suited to me. But I realise that would be a futile search if I were to embark upon it. Outside this Community I would not be able to attain that which my heart desires. My desires cannot be satisfied completely either here within the cloister or anywhere else unless I look first and foremost to the Saviour. Only within Christ is there the fullest possibility to enjoy the abundant life proclaimed in the Gospels.

Being firmly attached to my brothers-in-Christ is the best antidote to the fragmentation that comes from never settling in thoroughly where I am. Upon examination of the vow of stability I've come to understand that it is expertly designed to quiet my restless wandering. There have been times when I've looked around and thought that everyone else's personal relationships were better than my own. So too I've known times when the acquisition of material possessions seemed a rewarding way to squeeze the maximum amount of personal enjoyment out of life. How easily my eyes stray and how quickly my attention is distracted from its rightful focus.

I suspect that to each of us there comes a day when our job, our home, our town or our family seem incredibly irritating and woefully deficient. Likewise there are times when we regret some of the decisions that we've made in life. We may lament not having chosen alternatives that we think would have been more rewarding than the current paths on which we are trudging our way through a daily grind that can seem unbearable. That has been my experience, but now I appreciate better how stability enables me to outlast the dark and cold places of life until the warming thaw comes. Then once again I can see new buds springing forth in those parts of life that previously had seemed absolutely barren. For this to happen I must wait patiently in company with the other members of my Community whenever the harsh winters of life come bringing their frozen assaults against me. Eventually spring will arrive and bring its spiritual renewal.

The three days of retreat immediately before my admission as a novice afforded me an opportunity to reflect on this without any disturbances. Lodged in the Annexe, a separate building adjacent to the Retreat House, those several days were spent in silence. Upon returning later to my room in the House of the Resurrection I felt a strong sense of gladness at being back amongst the brethren. I'd already begun to think of them as "my brothers" even though officially I had not yet been admitted into their ranks. That three-day retreat made me aware of how much I missed their company. After my admission as a novice several of the monks greeted me with enthusiastic smiles saying *"Welcome brother."* I really had the feeling of being at home with this collection of people who have come to form a special sort of family for me. Like me they have their quirks and foibles. However within each of them there is something that I find appealing and endearing, and it is to them that I have made a commitment to walk upon life's pilgrimage as we journey together in the company of our Lord Jesus Christ.

With this assemblage of people I am experiencing the transformation that is essential for spiritual development and growth. This does not fall automatically and effortlessly into my lap, and daily I am discovering ways in which I must dedicate myself anew to the pursuit of rebirth. My own commitment to this process is not, in and of itself, sufficient to enable my faith to come to fruition. For that to happen I need the help of my brothers residing with me in this Community.

Stability ought not to be something sought only by nuns and monks. It is applicable to all Christians and spiritual health depends upon it. Regardless of whether one is single or married, living within the walls of a cloister or in the secular world, stability is a building block upon which our growth and maturation are dependent. This requires working things out and going on no matter what our personal feelings or frustrations may be at any one moment. This is not an easy endeavour, and I confess that there have been times when I've been tempted to "throw in the towel" and call it quits with this experience of communal living. Fortunately after prayerful reflection God brings me to a realisation that everything in life cannot be easily cured, instantly resolved, or painlessly eliminated. Some things simply have to be accepted, bravely borne and patiently endured before we can come to a state of joy and peace.

The commitment that I made to become part of the Community of the Resurrection is not unlike those of other commitments that people make to their spouse, their partner, their children, their parents, their employers and others with who they are in a relationship. Obligations are chosen and the corresponding duties are accepted as part of our commitment to those relationships. This may seem constricting to our personal freedom but the wonderful paradox is the enhancement of life that we gain. Renouncing our personal freedom to get up and leave at any time enables us to explore more deeply the place where we are and the other people with whom we sharing this life. This permits us to send down deep roots, to let something grow and reach maturity, and to produce fruit.

I find myself praying for perseverance because the desired fruits that are the products of our faithful commitment do not come easily. Through the clarity of hindsight I see that it is the relationships with my brothers here that are the strengthening supports sustaining me on those days when I am down and feeling the need of assurance or comfort from another person. The Constitutions of this community, in referring to stability, assert that "This commitment rests on the belief that such a life, in a house whose priority is the worship and service of God, is itself a witness to the Gospel."[31] The brethren of the Community of the Resurrection are striving to live in a manner that is shaped by the Gospels. It sounds so simple but in reality it is incredibly hard work. Sometimes we grate upon each other's nerves and fray one another's tempers as we interact within the confines of these walls in which we dwell. Abbot Stuart Burns, of Mucknell Abbey, states that "when the almost overwhelming temptation is to assume that it is all a big mistake, and we feel ready to throw in the towel and give up, this is precisely the moment to stay put and explore the invitation to growth."[32] The fleshing out of a Christ-centred lifestyle amidst this collection of seemingly incompatible people makes it apparent that God's grace is needed if we are to have any hope of succeeding in honouring our mutual commitments.

Stability, as measured through steadfastness to my brothers, also is a measure of love. In my relationships with the other brethren I find a

---

[31] CR Constitutions, p. 40.
[32] Graham Cray et al,
    New Monasticism as Fresh Expression of Church, p. 144.

fullness of life that is much more than the shallow satisfaction of my selfish wishes and desires. Within my vowed stability to this Community I am learning about the profound depths of love that is beyond physical gratification. For love to be more than a fleeting mixture of emotional attraction and anatomical arousal it must be able to withstand the long days when there seems to be no affectionate spark at all. It must be formed of sincere friendship, nurtured by mutual respect, and grounded within spiritual integrity. If those ingredients are not present then it will not survive the stresses and strains that life throws against it. This is true not only for those professed to celibacy but also for those in covenanted relationships like marriage. Such wholehearted commitment involves being called from the selfishness of individualism into the connectedness that comes from a sacrificial love demonstrated by faithful commitment to another person.

It is the faithfulness of God that enables me to keep going back to face the difficult parts of life. The simple truth is that I am not keeping the monastic vows through the merits of my own strength. So too a married couple cannot honour their vows to one another by relying on their own resources. I am able to uphold my commitment to my brethren only through the grace of God who is present at every moment of life as the supportive and sustaining Source of all that I am and hope to be. God is the one who makes my continued commitment to the Community of the Resurrection possible.

Stability is an important element in enabling the continuing revelation of God to be revealed within daily life. If I were to pack my bags and walk out of this place on the next occasion of distress or discomfort then I would miss the opportunities to encounter God through my brethren. I must see this monastic journey through to its earthly end. If I want to learn what it is that God intends for me then I must be on hand to receive the insights whenever such revelations come – even when those manifestations of the Divine come via persons whom I regard as rather unlikely channels of such grace. Stability lets me engage in an exploration of the face of God hidden in its transcendence yet revealed in the lives of these brethren amongst whom I dwell. It is here that I must remain because it is within this company of brothers that I have the best prospects of coming to be all that I am intended by God to be in life.

Chapter 7: Fully Engaged

After many years of living independently as a single person communal life is a considerable challenge for me. No longer do I answer to myself alone. I know that I cannot truly love God without loving my fellow human beings, but sometimes the reality of this is not nearly as easy to practise as the cognitive embrace of the theory. As St. John's first epistle says, "those who do not love a brother or sister whom they have seen, cannot love God whom they have not seen. The commandment we have is this: those who love God must love their brothers and sisters also."[33] The scriptural mandate seems quite clear: it is incumbent upon Christians to love others. The self-centred life of narcissism is not an option for anyone professing to love God. Whenever you become preoccupied with trying to "Be yourself" in a personally-driven quest for individual fulfilment then you need to step back and remind yourself that Jesus says "Be with me!" It is only within intimate union with Christ that we can be our true self. Ironically when we lose ourselves completely in God then we find our true self.

Stereotypes abound portraying a monastery as a place of seclusion in which its inhabitants live in quiet isolation from all but the most minimal sort of contact with anyone else. The reality is that life within a monastery does not remove one from contact with other people. Daily I am confronted with the challenge of living my faith amidst the company of seventeen other men of diverse personalities. As I interact with them my weaknesses are revealed through the ways in which I fall short of living fully within an attitude of love. This is especially evident when another brother's idiosyncratic habits annoy me or his peculiar quirks distract me to the point where I begin thinking uncharitable thoughts. At such times my irritation does not manifest the generous love of my neighbour to which I am being called by God. S.J. Forrest's limerick entitled *"Love All"* conveys the challenge of putting into practice the Gospel mandate to love others.

> The problem, when speaking of charity,
> Is how to define it with clarity
> For between the ideal

---

[33] 1 John 4:20-21

And the actually real,
We notice a certain disparity.[34]

Prior to my arrival I'd viewed the Community of the Resurrection through an idealistic lens. Only the sanctity of its members was seen and their humanity was barely noticed. Upon entrance I soon discovered that there was a disparity between my pious ideal and the "actually real" life of these men of widely different personalities living together in close company. Entering a religious community has not removed me from contact with real people or the real world. In fact I find myself confronted with harsh realism to an even deeper extent because of the constant face-to-face interactions that are an unavoidable part of living together. The intensity of our shared life can result in friction and irritation, but as Martin Israel says: "An emotional life devoid of anger would be tepid and unreal. Where there was no anger there might be no strong affection either; relationships would amount to the exchange of pleasantries and a moderate overall goodwill, but with little commitment to put oneself to any trouble in helping a fellow creature."[35] The whole panoply of human emotions, including anger, is present within this community. However in each person there also is a clearly detectable core of strong affection. It is this foundation of love for one another as individuals, and for God whom we strive to worship and serve, which is the adhesive that holds together this motley collection of men.

Sometimes the disparity between the ideal and the reality of our behaviour is disconcerting because it shatters the pretences of piety. Looked at from afar the monastic life may seem as though its entire existence is composed of serene sanctity. Upon closer inspection it is apparent that the interpersonal dynamic of harmony with one's brothers or sisters is not always found within the cloister. Initially there was something very appealing about the unique "separation" of the monastic life that resonated with me. As an introverted person I was attracted by the quietness, solitude, inwardness, orderliness and peace that I'd experienced whenever visiting monastic communities. Upon entering I discovered that those attributes are elusive to attain and also difficult to maintain once achieved.

---

[34] S.J. Forrest, *Love All* in Parson's Play-pen, p. 55.
[35] Martin Israel, Night Thoughts, p. 34.

The element of withdrawal that is characteristic of traditional monasticism exerted a powerful appeal to the romanticised spirituality of the "holy life" that I desired. With a naive earnestness that propelled my vocation, and an ardour inspired by heroic examples of saintly witnesses, I believed that I was ready to renounce my egocentric self and take up the cross in service of the Saviour. Despite the sincerity of my intentions I fell into the trap of placing an emphasis on the acts that I would perform. Simultaneously I avoided bringing the Gospel to bear upon my life through loving those standing right beside me.

It should not be surprising to discover that life behind the cloister walls reflects the same dynamics that are occurring in the hustle and bustle of the world. Even monks and nuns still are "in" this world even though trying not to be people "of" the world. The 21st century is characterised by an increasingly disordered, fragmented and secularised culture. With the general collapse of social altruism and its replacement by the avaricious pursuit of material prosperity, compounded by the insanity of individualism pursued to the point of hedonism, and the escalating spiral of technological and sociological madness that is endemic within much of contemporary culture, the stark contrast of the monastic life draws a fair number of enquirers and seekers. In many ways it is an attractive alternative to the frenzy that pervades our hectic human existence in this current century.

Although clearly counter-cultural in myriad ways none the less the monastic life isn't a non-stop experience of other-worldly holiness lived on a lofty spiritual dimension within the sheltering walls of a hallowed place. There are numerous practical tasks needing to be done and some of them are undeniably less-than-enjoyable chores. During the performance of these mundane activities a variety of interpersonal conflicts can arise. One of Mirfield's monks touched on this in his commentary upon our Rule: "The novice sometimes learns, to his surprise, how ordinary, indeed how commonplace, is the daily life at the Mother House. If he has dreamed of hours of absorbing prayer or spiritual converse with holy seniors, he finds instead cups to be washed, corridors to be swept, and brethren after all not so holy."[36]

It did not take me long to notice significant differences between the ways in which I had exercised my priestly vocation within a parish in comparison to the monastic setting. Previously I had enjoyed the status

---

[36] Hubert Northcott, Commentary on The Rule, p. 14.

and deference accorded to me as the "top dog" within the hierarchy, but at Mirfield every monk is expected to serve their turn as the "chief cook *and* bottle washer." As a parish priest I had a guild of women who tended to the vestments, washed and ironed the linens, arranged the flowers, and adorned the altar as a place of beauty. Now I have been doing some of those tasks, and I regret to say that my floral arrangements have not been the works of art that I'd known in the past when more skilful hands were involved.

In the past whenever I'd wanted something posted to a group of parishioners, the secretary in the church office would do the mail merge programme and collate everything together. Now I am faced with learning how to get a computer to produce such things for me. Polishing the brassware and silverware, cleaning up candle wax, and setting up for the liturgies are tasks in which I am engaged. So too I've been running the Hoover over the chapel's carpets, whilst in parish life I had a sexton who was responsible for cleaning the premises. Previously I had a cadre of youthful acolytes who ensured that the charcoal was ignited and burning properly before the thurible was brought to me to be sprinkled with the grains of incense, but now I've had to do these pyrotechnic procedures myself.

Once when I was carrying a tray of cups through the front hall into the refectory I overheard one guest saying to another, "I couldn't see myself being content to stay here and do this year after year." At a casual glance the mundane nature of our tasks may seem tedious and unrewarding. Certainly we lack the glitz and glamour of a television evangelist whose charismatic showmanship grabs people's attention. But the monastic life is not about what grand things we do. Instead it is about *living* in the fullness of God's call. Day after day, year in and year out, nuns and monks – indeed all Christians – are invited by God to live the abundant life at every moment. No matter how challenging, irritating, exhausting or delightful those moments may be for us we are called to enter into them with our whole self.

Sometimes the presence of God is subtly disguised in raking leaves, sweeping floors, washing dirty dishes, doing the laundry, cleaning up an infirm brother's bowel movement or myriad other chores. In each one of our tasks there is the possibility for us to encounter the Divine. Brother Roger, the founder of Taizé, said: "Following Christ with a steadfast heart does not mean lighting fireworks that flare up brightly and then go out. It means setting out, and then remaining, on a road of

trust that can last our whole life. This trust always remains humble."[37]
Few of the activities in which I engage are spectacular, and fireworks
don't flare up in a brilliant panoply proclaiming what I am doing daily
as a monk. Yet even the most ordinary activities are opportunities for
me to meet God.

One aspect that endows monastic work with a special character is
our effort to be fully present in whatever occupation we are engaged.
I've found it much easier to be invested in the tasks that I like and
enjoy, and more difficult to pour myself into those chores that I loathe.
A remedy that has assisted me in overcoming my reluctant engagement
in tasks that I dislike is the example set by the brethren. From the
beginning I was impressed by seeing the Superior and all the other
able-bodied members cleaning, scrubbing, dusting, washing, raking,
pruning and doing all sorts of manual work. The sight of everyone
taking a turn clearing the tables after meals and in the kitchen washing
the dishes made me realise that we are all in this together. I am not
alone in doing these tasks, and here amongst my brothers I've come to
understand more about God's love as revealed within the
companionship experienced in shared chores. This mutuality of
journeying with my monastic brothers as we engage in our daily work
is both an essential function and a blessing of communal life.

I used to think that God wanted me to change the world through the
activities in which I was to participate. The reality is that God
primarily is interested in changing me! Over and over I've had to learn
how to "step back" and not dive into something. Initially I thought that
through my efforts I could be the spiritual rescuer of others. I was
oblivious to how desperately I needed God to rescue me. Now I am
discovering the importance of letting God set the agenda and be in
control. "More often than not we do too much because we are afraid of
being judged as failures, we do not trust others to do their share, we
wish to exclude alternative approaches, or we want to ensure that we
remain unchallenged in the driver's seat."[38] In that quotation, Michael
Casey accurately summarised the reasons why oftentimes I am keen to
do something and have plunged headlong into a project.

My participation in this communal life depends on my ability to let
things be what they are for me and for every other person. I must not

---

[37] Brother Roger of Taizé, God Is Love Alone, p. 26.
[38] Michael Casey, Strangers to the City, p. 34.

strive to make this place or its inhabitants conform to my own particular ideals. Both the gifts and the limitations of others must be accepted. Through the struggles and frustrations of daily living we acquire the most enlightening insights about the fullness of life of which humanity is capable. This involves the realisation that everything won't always be done to our liking. We are given ample opportunities to learn that life still can be very good even when things are not performed according to our personal pleasure.

Monastic work is like every other sort of human labour in that it is partly enjoyable and partly disagreeable. No matter where one lives the reality of work needing to be done affects all of us. Even with a positive attitude it may not be possible to convert every task or chore into an activity of enjoyment. There also can be a penitential aspect to work. This may form part of the process of spiritual renewal and transformation as we become co-workers with Christ in sowing the seeds of the Kingdom of God. Within monasticism this is reinforced by the vow of obedience whereby a nun or a monk is bound to daily fidelity in whatever assigned tasks the community determines need to be done.

The saying "It's a dirty job but somebody has to do it" applies to monastic life because here too there are unpleasant chores that must be done by someone. Daily life for each of us brings with it a certain degree of messiness, and although some of these messes may smell quite nasty none the less they need to be cleaned up. Fortunately we have the assurance of knowing that our efforts are regarded as being fruitful even when our labours fail to bring results measurable by the standards of worldly achievement and success. Whenever we do our tasks as part of God's gracious will then we are participating in the Kingdom of God and eventually we shall reap the spiritual fruits of our labours.

Chapter 8: Close Encounters of the Divine Kind

The world is full of empty chatter, hollow talk, easy confessions, insincere compliments and glib confidentialities. Noise surrounds us and oftentimes silence is elusive. The modern tendency is to run away from confronting our inner self by looking constantly for distractions to divert our attention and entertain us. In contrast I was propelled upon my monastic explorations by a conviction that the quest to live an authentic Christian spirituality is worth all the efforts involved in leaving even the most attractive "noise" of the world and pursuing the challenging endeavour of communal living within religious vows.

From the moment of my first visit to Mirfield over a dozen years ago I was struck by the pervasive sense of peace that imbues this place. The Constitutions of the Community assert that "Brethren shall seek to make the houses of the Community places of stillness and recollection,"[39] and that is precisely what I found when I arrived here. Monks and nuns spend quite a lot of time in stillness and solitude. This is not done for self-centred reasons but to deepen affection for others because silence serves as the meeting place wherein real community becomes possible. Superficial conversation does not create or nurture a spirit of community. The endless chatter of mindless talk merely fills up the void of a silent space. In solitude we encounter the Christ who embraces us and offers us the freedom to love because he first loved us.

Henri Nouwen, in his book *Reaching Out*, states: "The solitude that really counts is the solitude of the heart; it is an inner quality or attitude that does not depend on physical isolation. On occasion isolation is necessary to develop this solitude of heart, but it would be sad if we considered this essential aspect of the spiritual life as a privilege of monks and hermits."[40] Every Christian is meant to be attentive to the 'still, small voice of God.' Such encounters with the Divine are not intended to be the exclusive preserve of nuns and monks. The busy, boisterous commotion of the world need not prevent you from encountering God, because the Lord is present within this world inhabited by divinity through the miracle of the incarnation. Nouwen explodes the fallacy of an artificial, self-induced quietude as being necessary for the spiritual life when he writes: "A real spiritual life …

---

[39] CR Constitutions, p. 37.
[40] Henri J. M. Nouwen, Reaching Out, p. 16.

makes us so alert and aware of the world around us that all that is and happens becomes part of our contemplation and meditation and invites us to a free and fearless response."[41]

Today it seems that everything is expected to be instant. People feel that nothing unpleasant should be endured and gratification must be immediate. We are not content to wait quietly in stillness for the hushed voice of God. Instead we expect our desire for intimate communion with God to be satisfied in the moment at which we want it to occur. Our spiritual timetable has come to resemble the rest of our world, and this is not surprising when one considers the ways in which we are preoccupied with the "now" moment. We are a society of microwave ovens, instantly available food, and same-day medical procedures. Advertisements tell us that we need not tolerate a cold or a headache or indigestion because some sort of pill is available to provide instantaneous relief from our ailments. We have become conditioned to receive results whenever we want them, which usually means immediately because we lack the patience to wait.

The message of the cross is contrary to what we're being taught by our culture around us. Suspended in the air from the ceiling in the monastery church hangs a large cross. It provides visual assurance that we too can rise to a newness of life if we endure and keep watch with Christ. Much of monastic life involves patiently waiting and watching for the Saviour. The cross of Jesus serves as a powerful reminder to all Christians that we can move forward through the most difficult experiences of life. We can triumph by never giving up on God who is our hope of salvation. When something seems nearly impossible, and giving up seems imperative, we are called to continue resting confidently in the arms of God who sustains us and enables us to persevere.

Too often we want to encounter God in the moment that is most convenient for us. We want God to be at our beck and call, and we assume that the reverential stillness in which we meet the Divine will happen automatically. In the 21st century world, where stimulation is omnipresent and noise of various types is constant, it takes determination to foster an environment of silence. It is easy to see the difficulties of finding a quiet place in which to meet God within the secular world, but monasteries are presumed to be locations where

---

[41] Ibid, p. 28.

such peace exists naturally and effortlessly. This is not true because even within the cloister there are noises pouring forth: the clinking of dishes, the clanking of pots, the wheezy humming as carpets are cleaned, and in this old building the creaking of floor boards and squeaking doors. Additionally there are the sniffles, sneezes, coughs, burps and farts that emanate from the brethren and break into the silence. At the House of the Resurrection we also have our silence broken by noise from the trains that pass through town, by cars and buses on the street alongside our grounds, and by jet planes travelling to the international airport in nearby Leeds. So even here silence is a privilege and not something that is taken for granted.

No matter how difficult it is to achieve silence, its attainment is important. We cannot commune very well with God if we are chattering unceasingly. Henri Nouwen recognised this when he wrote: "Somewhere we know that without silence words lose their meaning, that without listening our speaking no longer heals, that without distance closeness cannot cure."[42] Our holistic wellness requires occasional opportunities for silence, and this is one of the gifts that monastic communities offer to the world.

At the Community of the Resurrection we observe silence from immediately after Compline until nine o'clock the following morning. That is a span of nearly twelve hours of unbroken silence. This is increased by further occasions of silence at various times, such as at certain meals which are eaten without talking. Furthermore some places are reserved as silent areas, such as the church and the library. Much of our day is spent in silence, and this characteristic of our life has become very important to me. I cherish the opportunities that such times provide for me to get to know myself more fully, with all that this discloses as I open myself to delving deeply into the interior space of the soul.

Maybe silence seems boring to you and you're wondering how you could tolerate such a quiet existence? Genuine silence is not an empty, wasted gap in an otherwise productive day – and that is true not merely for nuns and monks but for all Christians. Whenever silence involves a state of attentiveness in which we hold ourselves ready to hear God speaking, then it is immensely beneficial and incredibly productive.

---

[42] Henri J. M. Nouwen, Out of Solitude, p. 14.

Silence gives me the space to read the signs of the times so that I can hear what the Holy Spirit is saying. In this way silence facilitates my own availability to others because it helps me to see and absorb what is happening. Silence also is a tool that teaches me to pray by holding myself in an attitude of attentiveness and receptivity to God in whose presence I am being still. Everyone needs to find an appropriate time and the right place in which to retreat into silence at least occasionally in order to commune with God. In a household full of children or teenagers perhaps this entails getting up early before the rest of the family awakens – or maybe using the locked door of a bathroom to ensure an uninterrupted time for prayer?

The monastic vernacular traditionally has referred to one's individual room as a "cell." Although that terminology is seldom used at Mirfield, we still regard our bedrooms as much more than places in which to sleep. Within this closely confined collection of brethren living together under one roof, the "cell" is a necessary element of solitude for our communally focused lives. As the sole area of private living space that I possess, my room is the place where I am most fully revealed for who I really am. The way that I treat this particular space is important because it can be the place where I encounter intimately the presence of God.

The appearance of my room says a great deal about the spiritual health of my walk with Christ. Whilst it is permissible for a monk's or a nun's room to reflect something of its inhabitant, yet it should not be cluttered with bric-a-brac or memorabilia. Not only do such collections of trinkets have a tendency to grow larger without our noticing their expansion, but they also can serve as distractions from the focused prayer and study for which we are called to use our rooms. The simplicity of a carefully arranged room, characterised by neatness and orderliness, is more than merely an aesthetic wish. I've heard it said by one of my monastic brothers that "If we don't meet God in our room, then we won't meet God anywhere else."

Facing myself and my Creator within my room sometimes is comforting and at other times excruciating, but it always turns out to be an enriching experience provided that I do not run away from the challenge of the confrontation. The Cistercian monk Charles Cummings wrote: "In the solitude of the cell, the monk or nun encounters God. The monastic cell is the abbey...reduced to its essential components: solitude, silence and the Spirit of God."[43]

I need to balance my times of personal retreat with those of community engagement. Within the solitude of my room I am enabled, by intimately encountering God's grace, to come to a profound sense of who I am as a beloved child of God. At the same time through sharing love with my brethren I also discover my true self. Both the individual and the communal dimensions are necessary components for my spiritual development, and they are interwoven together. Within solitude I discover the truth about my inner self that I can share during the course of my interactions with others. I am discovering that I can be solitary without being lonely. Even within the isolation of my room I am always in the intimate presence of God. In my room, sitting in prayer with my eyes closed and my heart open, I have felt the warmth of God's cheek touch mine with a tender caress, our noses rub together in affection, and my lips brushed gently with a superlative love that melted me to tears.

The presence of God in my room is reinforced visually by the crucifix that hangs on the wall in a position of prominence. Traditionally every cell of an abbey or convent contains a crucifix displayed prominently somewhere within the room. According to Cummings, "The crucifix on the wall is a reminder that the cell is filled with the presence of Christ and is not merely an empty space where a person sits alone with himself."[44] Whenever I sit in the upholstered chair that is in my room I am facing towards the wall on which hangs a cross of wood with a brass figure of Christ. Meditating upon that image each morning as part of my private devotions, I remember being amazed the first time that I experienced the phenomenon of its being inwardly imprinted upon me. I'd been gazing intently, almost trancelike, at it for quite some time. During the course of my contemplation I closed my eyes. To my surprise the image of the cross remained there before me even though my eyelids were closed, but the colours were reversed like a photograph's negative film. Instead of a dark cross upon a white wall, now I was seeing a black wall illuminated by a glowing white cross.

---

[43] Charles Cummings, Monastic Practices, p. 154.
[44] Ibid, p. 157.

There have been times of spiritual distress when I've knelt on the floor and gazed up at that cross upon my wall. Within those "dark nights of the soul," when I've felt far away from God, it is a comfort to encounter the presence of Christ's cross seared on my interior vision even when my eyes are closed. Every time that this happens to me I offer my prayerful thanksgiving to God for keeping the cross always in my line of sight.

Taking time to draw apart from the world's frenzied pace, and all that consumes our energies in life, is vital to our spiritual health. Retreating in order to move forward is an odd notion when viewed from a military perspective, but pulling back from hectic activities in order to recharge spiritual batteries is very important. It is easy to wear yourself down from striving always to press ahead and move forward, but it is essential to take advantage of opportunities to retreat into God's presence. Therein is where we can connect with God's strength and find the resources to continue engaging in serving Christ. A monastery offers a quiet environment in which to retreat for the recharging of a person's spiritual batteries. This poem, featured in an article by Bill Crowder within *Our Daily Bread*, nicely expresses this theme:

"To face life's many challenges
And overcome each test,
The Lord tells us to take the time
To stop. To pray. To rest."[45]

An absolutely perfect place in which to retreat to enter into an awesome experience of divine peace is impossible to find. There is no location within one's house or office that is ideal at all times of the day or night, and I've already described how the serenity of our monastic buildings periodically is interrupted by circumstances that break the stillness of our environs. A perfect religious community is a romanticised fiction. But a religious order does not have to be perfect in order to be a place wherein wholeness and holiness can be discovered. The Community of the Resurrection is a spiritually healing salve for my soul even though I live in an environment filled with those who exasperate and irritate me. No doubt I also bring similar frustrations to them. None the less it is here amongst them that I am meant to experience the love of God.

---

[45] Bill Crowder, *Retreating Forward* in Our Daily Bread, not paginated.

Monastic spirituality is teaching me that I must live in the midst of the human struggle rather than trying to avoid or escape from it. Daily I am realising that living in this community is an expression of human asceticism, because to live here involves undergoing the painful process of having the edges rubbed off me as the rough parts of my personality are made smooth. These experiences of abrasion are neither pleasant nor comfortable, but they are part of the discipline of the vowed life and they are a means of bringing about growth and maturity for me. A genuine sense of community arises from within a context where the sharing of pain takes place. It is through the experiences of struggling – with myself, with my brethren, and with God – that I enter more fully into the intimacy of communion.

I discovered quite quickly that a monastery is not an entirely peaceful place either by nature or by chance. No matter how much I, or any of the other monks, desire to give ourselves to God we still remain distinctly our unique selves. Inevitably these individual selves grate against one another. This tendency is magnified by being 'cloistered' within relatively confined spaces that force us to keep encountering the very same people again and again.

It is a monastery's intentional peace that provides its best chance for deep prayer, and this enables us to grow into greater spiritual maturity. Despite the auditory distractions that I've mentioned, this is a place where stillness and serenity are treasured and protected. Based upon comments made by our numerous visitors this is one of the primary attractions of monasticism for our guests. This prayerful silence and peaceful serenity does not come easily. They require much care lest they are undermined by the many distractions that so easily could overturn a monastery's peace.

Fortunately the order and rhythm of each day creates an atmosphere which provides the spaces and occasions in which to meet and commune with God. The repetitive behaviours of monastic life affect and shape our personalities upon a conscious and a subconscious level. Spiritual growth occurs within the course of our participation in the flow of everyday living within this setting. For this growth to happen I must engage myself as fully as possible in the community of which I am an integral part.

Admittedly I do not always want to encounter God or my neighbouring brother. There are times when I am immersed in an activity and find myself resenting the need to cease from my unfinished task in order to go to church to meet God. How inconvenient God's appointed times can be for my own schedule! When entering the church in such an attitude I do not "feel" anything that could be labelled as spiritually edifying. Given my begrudging mood at those times is it any surprise that I do not experience a great spiritual awakening? How can I be overwhelmed by the presence of God if I am determined to erect a wall of resistance to the movements of the Spirit? Fortunately I've learned that I need to be there in the church with my brothers-in-Christ surrounding me. Even when my own mood is foul, my brothers carry me along with them into the presence of God. It is essential to be amongst them even when I don't really feel like it, because it is in the midst of them that I find myself encouraged and strengthened.

Are we so busy seeking an encounter of the divine kind that we overlook the opportunities that are staring us in the face? All around us are opportunities to encounter some dimension of the holy within our Christian brothers and sisters. As a personal admission I confess to exactly this sort of blindness. Countless times I've gone into the church to worship Jesus but never bothered to observe the ways that Christ is being reflected through my monastic brothers. Similarly I suspect that we are guilty of doing this with our spouse or partner, our children, other relatives, our colleagues and bosses, our neighbours, and the whole panoply of humanity whom we meet daily. How easily we miss seeing Jesus when he is portrayed in the face of the person who is right next to us!

We need regular contact with one another because it is through the mutuality of our interactions that we are given glimpses of the Creator. We also need occasions of solitude and silence. Both are part and parcel of being fully human. Neither the intimacy of marriage nor close friendships will take away our need for occasional solitude. Sooner or later we discover that even when we are in the midst of a great crowd of people there is a part deep within us that remains in solitude, and that is the sacred inner core to which God alone has access.

Chapter 9: Still Struggling To Pray

A common image of a monk or a nun is of a person sitting around with hours of totally unencumbered time engaging in prayer. That image was present in my own mind, at least to some degree, when I arrived in Mirfield. However I've been amazed at how rapidly the level of my household activities have increased. Even within my first few months some tasks were being assigned to me, and I was astonished to discover how easily the obligations of daily life greedily consumed my time. The leisurely hours filled with endless opportunities for prayer that I'd imagined as part of the monastic life have not materialised. Instead I am finding out that washing dishes, trimming candles, taking care of infirm brethren, shelving books in the library, stocking the bookshop, doing administrative work in the office, typing data into the computer, arranging accommodations for guests, and countless other tasks all eat away the hours before I even notice that they are being consumed.

Spiritual wellness requires me to step back from the busyness of life to hear the inner voice calling me back to the essentials of love. As Jean Vanier, founder of the *L'Arche* communities, says: "To pray is to be centred in love; it is to let what is deepest within us come to the surface. Prayer is also a meeting with the One who loves me, who reveals to me my secret value, who empowers me to give life, who loves us all, and who calls us forth to greater love and compassion."[46]

I once thought that becoming a monk would lead to my rapid development as a powerful prayer warrior deeply immersed in profound encounters with God. But here I am several years later and still struggling to pray. Now I realise that it is necessary for me to be very deliberate in setting aside time to commune with God in prayer. As Tom Wright, the bishop of Durham, said in a sermon upon the occasion of an ordination:

> "Of course prayer is often difficult. It wouldn't be worth much if it wasn't. Again and again other concerns crowd in and threaten to disrupt our praying. That is to be expected ....
> It gets harder, not easier, but part of the trick is to recognise that the difficulties are themselves a sign that prayer matters, that the enemy knows if he can prevent you from being

---

[46] Jean Vanier, Becoming Human, p. 32.

rooted and grounded in Christ and discovering the true wisdom in him he will have neutralised your effectiveness."[47]

In ways subtle yet subversive the cares and concerns of daily life crowd in upon our time and push aside our noblest intentions to preserve some prayerful time communing with God. You might think that nuns and monks would be immune to such distractions but we are just as prone to having our attention diverted from God as anyone else. Prayer is at the centre of the monastic life, at the very heart of all that we do, yet within religious communities it can be a struggle to keep a right focus upon the pre-eminence of prayer. So we keep trying, and failing, but even within our failure we are broken open to receive more of the gift of God's restorative grace.

Once a person enters into prayer it begins to work its own natural process of transformation. Little by little, bit by bit, we are touched until every part of our self and our life is affected by the Holy Spirit. Prayer cannot be separated from the other aspects of life. It has an unsettling way of knocking out the props that we've erected to protect our personal domain. If we are honest then we must acknowledge that there are areas that we do not want to hand over to God because we're happy with the way that we are managing them. Why would we choose to have our cosy areas of personal interest tampered with and transformed by God's interference? Don't most of us harbour a fear that God could ask us to relinquish some of the things to which we are fondly attached?

> "The call is continually to trust, to let go of control and be empty-handed before God, holding on to nothing for ourselves but clinging to him alone. My natural tendency is to hold the reins of control very tightly and to want to know the way ahead. In prayer I hear the invitation to surrender, to leave the props behind, and to fall into the hands of the living God."[48]

Surrendering oneself is a daunting prospect, and it is intimidating to ponder what is involved by falling into the hands of God. As one who held exactly those reservations, I was reluctant to let myself fall completely into the hands of the Almighty. I feared that a genuine encounter with God might lead to a reordering of my life along lines

---

[47] Tom Wright, The Anglican Digest, Winter 2009, p. 5.
[48] Laurentia, Touched by God, p. 22.

that would change what I had constructed with painstaking care over the course of my lifetime.

The rhythm of the monastic life provides a structural support for enabling me to surrender to God. The four-fold Daily Office is a priceless resource that assists me in placing myself in God's hands. These services and the Mass are not escapist occasions shut off from "real" life. They are the key points within our common life when God communicates to us. In reference to the Mass, the Benedictine sisters in West Malling say that the Eucharistic rite is "the creative love of God at work in the Christian, a spiritual presence of love going out to the uttermost parts of the earth and drawing together the hearts of all mankind. Here is the true union and communion transcending all barriers .... Here is the victory which overcomes the world, Christ's victory of love operative in the redeemed."[49]

Sometimes the events and intensity of life presents barriers preventing us from entering into the love that draws us to God and to one another. Our contemporary world is downright noisy, and we may wish for a soundproof shield within which we could enclose ourselves in order to commune prayerfully with God. But such a magical shield against exterior sounds still would not silence the internal noises that reverberate in our minds. Even within the relatively quiet environment of a monastery I find it difficult to enter the interior stillness where my cares and concerns, anxieties and worries, serious thoughts and whimsical daydreams do not intrude and distract my prayers. Of my own accord I am not able to overcome this dilemma, but God provides a way for me to quiet my heart by inviting me to exchange my cares for his peace. Only when I place my concerns in God's hands do I find inner quietness.

Despite my efforts to relinquish "my business" into God's hands, my thoughts are occupied with an array of issues that divert my attention from its rightful focus. Fortunately the rhythm of the Daily Offices channels me back to God when my mind wanders. The Offices are communal prayer, and since I am not as proficient at prayer as I ought to be these daily services are beneficial aids to my inadequate personal prayer life. In the Community of the Resurrection we use a four-fold Daily Office: beginning with Mattins, followed by the Mid-day Office, then proceeding on to Evensong and concluding with

---

[49] The Eucharist, West Malling, p. 4.

Compline. However the reality is that those four occasions are only part of the picture. The actual fact is that we are living our prayer-filled lives 24 hours a day, 7 days a week, and 365 days a year. This totality of personal investment is not something reserved only for nuns and monks. Every Christian is called to live within a realm of engagement with the Divine because there is no area of life that is not touched by God.

By praying with the brethren several times each day I am learning how to pray for the whole body of humanity. When my intercessions are joined with those of others then my prayers are broadened beyond a personal focus. In an article entitled *"Prayer"* William Willoughby wrote: "To insure that we do not go off on flights of fancy it is important that our prayer take place in the midst of a praying community gathered to listen to the Word of God and partake of our Lord's sacramental presence…. In community we become familiar with the words of Jesus and his prayer as they resonate in the Body of Christ."[50] I am prone to mental flights of fancy when endeavouring to prayer, so being in a praying community is helpful in keeping me focused and centred. Daydreams and distractions are less likely to gain a foothold in my thoughts when my words are joined aloud with my brothers as we pray according to the forms of our liturgy.

Prayer is very personal and arises from the heart, but it needs the support and protection of a nurturing Christian community in which to grow. Prayer is not an individualistic expression of a person's wishes and desires. It should be embedded within the life of a worshipping congregation in which one is a participant. This is important because within a community of faith is where we find the climate that sustains and deepens our prayer. Through prayerful interactions with others we are enabled to look beyond the narrow field of our own private needs. Having spiritual companions with whom to open one's heart and share life's experiences is an invaluable aid to the prayer journey. It is significant that the Christian community gathers together for prayer because by being there we are supporting one another's prayers. Our presence matters because in corporate prayer not only are we giving ourselves to God but we're also giving ourselves to one another.

Some people wonder why monks and nuns set aside so much time for prayer? These people question whether such an investment is

---

[50] William Willoughby,*Prayer* The Anglican Digest, Summer 2010, p. 36.

worthwhile when there are so many urgent needs demanding our involvement and intervention. Might our time be spent more profitably if we'd get up off our knees and go out into the trenches actively doing "real" ministry? To such enquiries I'd like to say that prayer *is* real ministry. It is not an esoteric endeavour restricted to the sacred confines of a spiritual dimension far above the heads of anyone else. Instead prayer is embedded within the commonplace realities of a religious community's work, worship and ministries.

Prayer is not a mind trip created by a carefully crafted formulary, because no instructional manual can prescribe a methodology for opening oneself to communion with God. In prayer it is better to have a heart without words than to have pious words without a heart desirous of receiving God. Some of my most meaningful occasions of prayerful intimacy have occurred when I've been carrying such heaviness or sadness that I cannot find words to express my pain. Opening myself to the presence of God, I cast myself into the loving arms of Jesus and surrender myself to his care whose embrace heals the wounds that I cannot even vocalise.

We are created to be in a relationship with God and prayer is the means by which that relationship is nurtured and sustained. When we take our relationship with God to an intimate level we find ourselves connected to the divine presence that knows us even better than we know ourselves. When we are in conversation with God there is no point in keeping any aspect of ourselves hidden. Even the most miniscule dimension of our personhood already is known to the Almighty. There is nothing about us that we can keep secret before the omniscient One.

The good news is that we always will find ourselves loved by God even though every wart and wrinkle of our souls is known with a clarity that oftentimes we have difficulty facing. One of my monastic brothers, in writing about prayer, has stated that "The influence of God in our prayers is the influence of truth upon the lies that we have created about ourselves. As [God's] loving influence penetrates our being, our masks and disguises begin to fall away and the true image of our real self is revealed."[51] Shedding the mask behind which I hide fills me with anxiety because there is a great vulnerability in revealing

---

[51] Simon Holden, Ways of Praying. Mirfield Publications, 1982, p. 1.

one's real self. Fortunately God values us for who we are and not for the eloquence of the words that we utter.

Given the nature of societal pressures it is easy to feel that we are of little worth if we are not able to rattle off an impressive list of things that we are doing. But God does not determine our value by how busy we are. Our worth to God is not based upon an evaluation of what we've accomplished. Living on the edge of exhaustion and not taking care of yourself is not the avenue leading to the abundant life to which Christ is calling. Too often we live at a furious pace so that the world will not leave us trailing behind in the dust. That may appear to be the route to worldly success but it is not the pathway leading to God's kingdom. Engaging in the activities that some regard as being "real ministry" might make you feel important or valuable, but what actually makes you important to God is not tied to any specific tasks that you are doing. Instead what is really important is what you allow God to accomplish within you when open to being transformed by his presence. As an anonymous poem says:

> Christ never asks of us such busy labour
> As leaves no time for resting at His feet;
> The waiting attitude of expectation
> He often counts as service most complete.[52]

Nuns and monks may not look 'productive' when evaluated from a perspective of worldly values, but the values of God's kingdom are not synonymous with those of the world. Every Christian is measured not by what they do for God but rather by what God is doing in them. Through prayer and contemplation one's intimate relationship with Christ is nourished and strengthened, thereby enabling effective engagement in all sorts of activities that promote the Kingdom of God. True contemplation, and the attendant process of moving inwards to the depths of our most sincere desires, does not isolate us from the reality that surrounds us. A healthy spiritual journey involves movement away from isolation towards harmony and union with ourselves, with other people, and with God. As one of my monastic brothers has said, "Prayer is not about consolation for ourselves, but about our hearts being changed, and about the growth of faith, hope and love in our lives."[53] There is no separation between praying and

---

[52] Julie Ackerman Link, *Keeping Busy?* Our Daily Bread, October 4th 2010.
[53] Simon Holden, Ways of Praying. p. 10.

living because they both flow into each other. Daily life is not punctuated occasionally by prayer because actually all of life itself becomes a prayer.

Chapter 10: Losing My Crutches

The monastic way offers an invitation that is simple yet profoundly challenging: to let go of individualistic striving and surrender entirely to God. This is not an endeavour that can be engaged in a half-hearted manner because it calls for a complete commitment. Although initially daunting when one considers the totality of this commitment, the result yields the rich harvest of a discovery of one's full humanity within the context of a community.

The totality of this commitment became clear to me with the removal of the comforting crutches of a "back-up plan" that I'd held as an escape route through which I could exit. At the time of my first profession in religious vows, the management and use my monetary assets was turned over to the Community of the Resurrection. The last financial crutches that had provided for me some sense of material security were knocked out from beneath me.

As the date of my first profession approached I grew frightened at the commitment that I would be making. Complete surrender was terrifying to contemplate, and some nights I was unable to sleep as I pondered the implications of taking this step that would lead me further towards permanent membership in this Community. In a song by Gloria Gaither and Bill George are these words referring to the offering of oneself to God: "Broken and spilled out and poured at your feet, in sweet abandon let me be spilled out and used up for thee."[54] Part of me desired to embrace that sentiment, yet another part was scared to death of such total surrender. I wanted to serve the Saviour but the prospect of being broken, spilled out and used up made me anxious. Being consumed by God, even by the sweetness of divine love, is so awesome that I could barely think about it. The way through this impasse was to remember that Jesus was broken and his blood was spilled out on Calvary's cross for love of me.

At the beginning of this book I wrote how I've come to find that one word expresses what motivates me to be a monk: Love. Small as that word looks when written it is enormous in its impact and awesome in its implications upon our lives. One of my favourite authors, Henri Nouwen, has written these eloquent words about the costly nature and the immeasurable rewards of loving.

---

[54] Gloria Gaither and Bill George, *Broken and Spilled Out,* lyrics to a song.

"Do not hesitate to love and to love deeply. You might be afraid of the pain that deep love can cause... but that should not hold you back from loving deeply... The more you have loved and allowed yourself to suffer because of your love, the more you will be able to let your heart grow wider and deeper... Yes, as you love deeply the ground of your heart will be broken more and more, but you will rejoice in the abundance of the fruit it will bear."[55]

When I commenced this journey of companionship with these monastic brethren I never imagined that surrendering to God in order to become my real self could involve so much pain and bring such intense hurt. The process of being broken open in complete abandonment to God has brought me to tears. At those times I resonate with the experiences of the Virgin Mary who opened herself to being fully within God's will, only to discover that such submission brought her to a painful place that pierced her heart with grief. Finding myself taken beyond the comfortable places in which I'd prefer to be resting, sometimes all I can manage to do is to gasp out a feeble "Yes" in response to God. Fortunately even my timid squeak of consent is enough for God to do the rest by transforming me through the grace of divine love.

The monastic call summons me daily to move beyond living in my head as it invites me to live from my heart, and sometimes I have found that to be an uncomfortable place in which to dwell. I am reluctant to leave my cerebral shelter because it is easier just being in my head. But God has thrown my previous balance completely off kilter. Broken and poured out, and left with an ache in my heart, the monastic life has opened up my vulnerability and thereby enabled me to venture deeply into myself and experience the love of Jesus.

Profession, as the term is used within monastic circles, is "the ceremony at which a Religious makes promises to live the Religious Life with integrity and fidelity to the Rule."[56] The solemn rituals of the liturgy of profession are symbolic in conveying that the new member is dying to the world and committing to spending the rest of one's life with the particular community amongst whom the person is making their vows. For me this occasion took place on 18th May 2012.

---

[55] Henri Nouwen, The Inner Voice of Love, p. 49.
[56] Anglican Directory of Religious Life, 2010-2011 Edition, p. 189.

Kneeling before the Superior, who stood in front of the altar, I made my first profession. Thereby I placed my whole self into God's hands for a journey, done in the company of these other monks, that ultimately shall lead us to our final home.

Profession itself is not an end in an absolute sense. Instead it marks the commencement of a lifelong pilgrimage pursued with the brothers or sisters with whom one is committing to walking as a companion. It is not the consummation of a spiritual journey, nor even a graduation from the stage of formation into that of greater maturity. As this Community's Constitutions say: "In profession we undertake a further dedication to realize our baptismal commitment to discipleship, accepting the particular opportunities and renunciations of the religious life as a true part of God's gracious call to us."[57] At a fundamental level the monastic pursuit is grounded in the baptismal covenant shared by all Christians, regardless of whether one's status is single or married, laity or clergy, monastic or secular. However it also is acknowledged that, as mentioned in the above quotation, there are some "particular opportunities and renunciations of the religious life" that are an essential part of monasticism.

Thanks to the popularity of the Franciscan movement many people are familiar with the three vows of "poverty, chastity and obedience" taken by those friars. A common assumption is that these are the words of monastic profession employed universally by all nuns and monks. The older Benedictine model uses different terminology, and its ancient formula is used by the brethren of the Community of the Resurrection. When I made my first profession I said these words aloud: "I solemnly promise before God and his saints, stability, conversion of life and obedience...."[58] In that statement I expressed my intention to throw away all of the crutches upon which I'd been dependent previously. Now I was committed to walking with this gathering of men amongst whom I have made my earthly home. The Constitutions of this Community elaborate upon that promise by explaining that "Through his profession each brother is committed to a life of consecrated celibacy, poverty and obedience."[59] It is these vows that I shall explore within the next three chapters.

---

[57] CR Constitutions, p. 10.

[58] Ibid., p. 6.

[59] Ibid., p. 10.

The Dominican archbishop William Barden has written: "We don't love God apart from loving God made man. We look into the eyes of our Jesus and there we see God. Lovers gaze into each others' eyes, and until we can look into the eyes of Christ we have not come to the end of the love story... All our Christian life with its ups and downs and failures and disappointments is all part of the love story."[60] Emotionally and spiritually there are numerous ups and downs in the monastic life, but even the potholes and rough patches are accepted because of the destination to which we are travelling. For the sake of this love story monks and nuns promise to adhere to certain disciplines of life. The reason why we embrace poverty, celibacy and obedience is because they are part of living into the incredible love story that leads us into deeper intimacy with the divine Lover.

---

[60] William Barden, *Dominican Life is a Tightrope*
in Religious Life Review, Vol 49, No 262, p. 182.

Chapter 11: Poor Yet Very Rich

The 21st century has a culture with an enormous appetite for immediate gratification, demanding satisfaction through the attainment and consumption of a vast array of consumer products. In contrast monastics deliberately choose a 'low-impact' lifestyle as a means of pursuing a spiritual life not distracted by a multitude of material possessions. This voluntary renunciation of the world's appealing conveniences is meant to be a pathway towards inner tranquillity, even though the perspective of Western capitalism regards it as woefully deficient and unrewarding. In the "world of plenty" inhabited by many Americans and Europeans, monastic spirituality can fill the inner emptiness and heal the spiritual brokenness of people. Amidst prosperity and material abundance such interior despair exists and it cries out for a remedy that the acquisition of more consumer goods cannot provide. As the character Mr. Lark says in a lament about contemporary American life: "Nobody seems happy anymore... Now that this country is so rich and overdeveloped, we have nothing to do but face the emptiness of life. We just drive cars and watch TV. Everybody's moving into gated communities and working on their abs. It's very narcissistic."[61]

I've left the 'worldly' life that I'd found to be filled with both excitement and stress, but I have not left the world itself because within the House of the Resurrection life's cares and concerns still exist. The brethren of the Community of the Resurrection are not trying to avoid life or run away from it. Instead we seek to live the ordinary life extraordinarily well by being in tune with the Spirit of God at work within the whole created order. You might think that a monastery in Yorkshire is a rather unlikely place from which to engage the world? Popular opinion thinks that a person who enters the monastic life is leaving the world, but we are deeply involved with the world's hurting people and their concerns.

Monastic life has given me a vantage point providing a different perspective from that usually seen by folks immersed in the world. When engaged in the pursuit of worldly goals it is possible to find oneself drowning in success. No longer am I buried beneath a clutter of material possessions. At the time of my profession in first vows I surrendered the right to control my own finances but no real

---

[61] Andrew Holleran, The Beauty of Men, p. 135.

diminishment has resulted from that action. Actually I've experienced the liberation involved in the recognition that money is not essential to the enjoyment of a rewarding life.

In 2009 I moved out of a beautiful four bedroom rectory situated on a charming tree-lined street in a posh residential neighbourhood. From that rectory I migrated to Mirfield where now I have only a bed, a desk, two chairs and storage for some clothes within this one room that forms the entirety of my private space within the House of the Resurrection. I enjoyed living in that comfortable house back in Pennsylvania, but I do not feel deprived now that my private domain has been reduced to a small fraction of the size of my former residence.

Having decided against the continuing pursuit of amassing more personal property, I've come to realise the spiritual bankruptcy of the consumer culture that I'd inhabited. Through the surrender of my personal possessions I have gained a privileged perspective from which to view the world with a clarity and insight I hadn't experienced before. The monastic lifestyle is not a new-fangled innovation because its origins are firmly grounded in the Scriptures. The opening sentences of this Community's Constitutions are explicit in rooting our life of material poverty upon a biblical foundation in imitation of the apostolic models provided by the earliest disciples of Jesus Christ:

> The Community of the Resurrection shall consist of men who, freely accepting the call of God, have made profession and vowed stability within the Community that they may follow the Gospel life after the pattern of those recorded in the Acts of the Apostles of whom it is said that 'they continued steadfastly in the apostles' teaching and in the fellowship, in the breaking of the bread and in the prayers' and 'the company of those who believed were of one heart and one soul, and no one said that any of the things which he possessed was his own, but they had everything in common.'[62]

Since its nineteenth century origins these brethren have sought to create a community formed and shaped by gospel values. We've declared our independence from the worldly values of society and have chosen different priorities as we strive to imitate Jesus Christ. These efforts are not based upon contempt for the present world, for within it

---

[62] CR Constitutions, p. 1.

we see the artistry of the Creator. Our hope is for transcending it in anticipation of the more wonderful world that is yet to come. The issue is not the worthiness of the actual items that exist within the world but rather how attached and dependent one so easily can become upon material goods that is the central concern for us.

Practising poverty makes my life less cluttered, and this in turn allows for more energy to be directed to seeking that divine communion for which I came to this monastery. Although it might sound like a marvellous windfall, an abundance of possessions actually is quite burdensome because of the care needed to maintain them and the anxiety that accompanies any potential loss of such wealth upon which we've placed our aspirations and entrusted our security. Henri Nouwen captured this sentiment in *Reaching Out* when he wrote: "Our society seems to be increasingly full of fearful, defensive, aggressive people anxiously clinging to their property and inclined to look at their surrounding world with suspicion, always expecting an enemy to suddenly appear, intrude and do harm."[63] Sadly that seems to be the life in which many affluent people are trapped as they are being held prisoner by material success that requires continual vigilance if it is to be protected and preserved.

Reducing one's attachment to possessions enables energy to be channelled in other directions that are liberating because they do not require maintaining a defensive posture of guarding accumulated assets. Again quoting Nouwen, "Once we have become poor, we can be a good host. It is indeed the paradox of hospitality that poverty makes a good host…. We only perceive the stranger as an enemy as long as we have something to defend."[64] Monks and nuns have nothing valuable of their own to defend. As a result, having nothing to lose we can be open to welcoming others without anxiety over preserving intact our material goods.

Poverty does not always have a positive connotation. It can be evil when it entails hunger, oppression, desperation, slavery, human trafficking or death. That is the awful face of poverty which cannot be condoned, and those dreadful conditions are not part of monastic life. The poverty of those professed in the religious life involves a deliberate simplification based within the recognition that God alone

---

[63] Henri Nouwen, Reaching Out, p. 43.
[64] Ibid., p. 74.

supplies all of our needs. As such it means relying on God's gifts for a healthy and balanced life in accordance with the fullness and abundance desired by God for creation. An abject state of material destitution is a misperception of the vow of poverty taken at profession by nuns and monks. As Brother Roger wrote in *The Rule of Taizé*, "The spirit of poverty does not consist in pursuing misery, but in setting everything in the simple beauty of creation."[65]

A genuine embrace of the monastic ethos of poverty focuses upon the voluntary and conscientious choices necessary for practising a reasonable simplicity of life. In striving not to be entrapped by the tempting allure of modern conveniences decisions have to be made daily about what sorts of appliances and technology to utilise. Part of this is about nothing more than the need to live within a budget. But our desire to exercise good stewardship over our communal property also harmonises with various environmental goals such as reducing one's carbon footprint in order to lessen humanity's impact upon the ecological habitats of the earth.

One example that comes to mind involves the electric drying machines in the laundry at the House of the Resurrection. Our custom is that elderly or infirm brethren can use them, while able-bodied brethren are supposed to carry their laundry outside in fair weather or downstairs to the cellar where they can dry by the heat from the furnace. Initially I regarded this as a tiresome inconvenience, and I considered it unreasonable since some perfectly functional tumble dryers were staring at me in the laundry room. They already were there, I said to myself, so why not use them? If I hadn't lived previously as a missionary in Africa for several years, where all laundry was done entirely by hand, I'd probably have rebelled outright against this policy.

The passage of time has proven to me the benefits and wisdom of not using something just because it happens to be available. The presence of an item does not mean that I have to employ it, and sometimes it is beneficial not to use something located near at hand. For instance your car may be parked in the garage and ready for immediate use, but isn't it a healthier choice (for you and for the environment) to walk the quarter or half a mile to the mailbox than to drive there in the car?

---

[65] Roger, The Rule of Taizé, p. 53.

Poverty for those within religious vows is not really about the lack of something. Instead it is concerned with learning to relax one's grip and willingly let go of things so that we can stand before God in simplicity. As the Community of St. Francis, in San Francisco, states: "For Francis poverty was more about *possession* than about *possessions* per se. In other words, our attitude toward our possessions is along the lines of the question 'Do we possess our possessions or do they possess us?'"[66]

Monastic poverty is not about being antagonistic to possessions and rebuffing all sorts of material items. That would be a skewed interpretation of what is intended by the vows. As a monk living in the United Kingdom, a nation that is relatively prosperous and possesses a developed economy, I am not residing within a milieu of debased impoverishment that suffers from the absence of modern appliances and technologies. I am not hungry, homeless and destitute. Indeed there are ample material goods surrounding me in every room of this monastery. Yet a lifestyle characterised by simplicity is a goal by which my brethren and I seek to live.

At the centre of the monastic vow of poverty is the desire to acknowledge everything as a gracious gift from the Creator. Accordingly everything is seen as belonging to God alone, and through the beneficence of the Almighty we are permitted to enjoy the use of many good gifts. It is paradoxical that the stripping and dispossession practised by monastics ends up being a way leading to immense richness and fulfilling abundance. It is not the sort of wealth easily measured by bankers whose definitions of assets are expressed in financial terms, but without a doubt I can say that the monastic life is a pathway to incredible spiritual richness.

---

[66] *Franciscan Poverty* The Anglican Digest Summer 2010, p. 53.

Chapter 12: What! No Sex?

Voluntarily chosen poverty is a counter-cultural value not readily embraced by many people in today's world, but I suspect that even such poverty is regarded more sympathetically and understood more easily than the vow of celibacy, also known by its traditional name of chastity. This vow seems almost impossible for people to comprehend, and they can barely fathom how a normal human being could live any sort of meaningful existence without sex.

As I begin this chapter let me say that since I am a human being I cannot help writing as a sexual person, and I fully affirm intimacy's worth and value. I believe that every one of us was born with a desire to relate to other human beings. A vital part of our humanity is that we are sociable as a species, and the need for intimacy with others is one of our deepest personal needs. We have a profound longing to come together so that we can touch, share in various forms of communion and be nurtured through the course of our interactions. Within intimacy the alienating expanse that separates us from others is bridged, and thereby we are able to know and appreciate better those with whom we are relating. As part of our natural need for love our body wants to be held and to hold others, to be touched and to touch others. It would be unhealthy for us to deny or repress these basic needs because they are a fundamental part of our created being.

I am engaged in pursuing a monastic vocation, but the fact remains that my need for intimacy is just as great as that of anyone else who resides outside the walls of a monastery. No less than everyone else, monks and nuns crave connectedness with other people within such realms as affection, camaraderie and shared enterprise. In the presence of those with whom I have an intimate relationship – and relationships need not involve sexual activity in order to be very intimate – I feel the liberating permission to be myself. Whenever we can be our real self and disclose fully our innermost being to another, then something incredibly rewarding matures within the context of that interpersonal environment of intimacy.

Due to the natural diversity of humanity, whereby every individual is unique, each person who embraces vowed celibacy travels on their own particular journey towards its attainment. At the risk of shattering the façade of sanctity that has been accorded to people who live the professed religious life, I want to state that monks and nuns do not become one-hundred percent chaste overnight. Instead we pursue this goal for our entire life, and I venture to say that it is only within the actual struggle to be chaste that one gradually is made chaste.

The monastic life is about much more than vowing to remain single. So too it entails more than merely refraining from genital and romantic activities. Celibacy includes both the physical and the spiritual aspects of being sexual. Thus it is intended to be affectionate, warm and emotional. If it were not able to contain those qualities within its interpersonal relationships then it could not survive because humans would find it impossible to remain committed to celibacy without such things that are the nurturing fruits of a healthy life.

Celibates are fully sexual people too. Now you may be thinking, "Wait a minute. How can that be true if you've promised to give up sex?" It is possible because sexuality is an inalienable part of our humanity, and a man or woman does not cease to be the sexual being of their original creation simply because they aren't actually "doing it" with another person. Perhaps one reason that we blush when articulating these thoughts about nuns and monks is from the embarrassment felt at acknowledging the persistence of sexual desires?

I suspect that few people make it through life without encountering occasions when our body seems to 'betray' us by reacting in ways contrary to what our minds regard as more proper than the physiological actions happening to us. Sometimes our bodies respond almost automatically with anatomical changes brought on by the appearance of someone attractive, yet having this natural reaction of bodily arousal does not mean that we've violated or abandoned our commitment of fidelity to either marital vows or a religious vocation. Those with the special calling to celibacy should neither fear nor denigrate the sexual dimension of an encounter with another person. Rather they ought to respect it and acknowledge that sexuality is more than a mere bodily response to whatever stimuli have caused excitement or arousal.

Celibacy is only one particular expression of life within the continuum of human sexuality with all of its diversity and variety. Within vowed celibacy nuns and monks voluntarily refrain from physical consummation with another individual in order to experience a greater depth of intimacy with all people. For monastics an authentic and healthy intimacy will not result in either obsession or exclusion. By first opening oneself to intimacy with God the monk or nun finds that others can be made more fully welcome. Paradoxically it is the commitment to celibacy that allows one to be relaxed and at ease around acquaintances, family, friends, guests and visitors, and with the spiritual sisters or brothers with whom one lives in community.

Celibacy is not really about isolation and aloneness. When correctly understood it concerns the inter-relatedness of persons expressed through an intentional commitment to forge deep connections with others in a manner that results in enriching and fruitful relationships. As *The Rule of Taizé* states, "If celibacy brings greater availability to concern oneself with the things of God, it is acceptable only in order to give oneself more fully to one's neighbour with the very love of Christ. Our celibacy means neither breaking with human affections nor indifference, but calls for the transformation of our natural love."[67]

Celibacy is possible as a lifelong commitment only when a person is motivated by an ardent spiritual desire sustained by God's grace. It is impossible to achieve such a lifestyle by reliance upon one's own internal resources. Celibacy is both a wonderful gift *and* an arduous task. It is a gift in that it is given and comes to fruition by God's grace. Simultaneously it is a task which a monastic must strive to fulfil each and every day. Celibacy is not sexual repression or the denial of one's sexuality because that would be denigrating our being created in God's image. According to Casey, "Genuine chastity, distinct from mere sexual abstinence, is built on truthfulness – accepting one's sexuality fully and attempting to integrate it into the whole fabric of personal, Christian and monastic existence." He goes on to say that chastity calls for "an acceptance of what we are by nature, who we are by personal choice, and what we might become when the grace of God works its way with us."[68]

Monastic spirituality is grounded in the importance of life shared with others. In this environment all of the members are to encourage, support, instruct, correct and learn from one another. The monastic testimony to this communal commitment to love is celibacy, whereby the nun or monk declares their belonging to everyone and yet at the same time to no one exclusively. Although this sounds contradictory yet it is a rewarding and enriching lifestyle. Celibacy proclaims that a healthy human community is built upon a great deal more than

---

[67] Roger, The Rule of Taizé, p. 47.
[68] Michael Casey, Strangers to the City, p. 55.

physical behaviours. Genuine community, expressed through communion with another person, is transcendent when it pours itself out to others without any expectation of a reciprocated outpouring from those who are the recipients.

The monastic promise of celibacy is lived in a context which provides boundaries that guide each member's behaviours, shape their values, and instruct their beliefs. To effectively sustain a healthy culture of chastity a monastic community must do much more than merely promulgate and enforce rules and regulations for celibacy's preservation. Fencing in sexuality with a lengthy list of rigid prohibitions enforced with harsh rigour is destined to result in failure because celibacy is not like a curio object in a museum that can be captured and contained for display within a glass case. For the proper formation of celibacy a religious community must be a place of acceptance, affirmation, friendship, and even a degree of intimacy.

Intimacy is created when I connect with another person without demanding that they be like me or different than they naturally are. It happens only when I am permitted to be my true self. Real intimacy cannot exist for long when smothered behind the mask of a false identity. Admittedly, within this context of interpersonal relating I do not always like some aspects of another person's behaviour or personality. I'm also sure that they do not like every idiosyncratic facet of my character either. None the less, through the solemn promises that I made when professed in this community, I committed myself to the challenging work of building and nurturing relationships with my monastic brothers. The primacy of these relationships within the wider life of the religious vocation is captured by the following quotation from the Trappist monk Thomas Merton:

> "Love in fact *is* the spiritual life, and without it all the other exercises of the spirit, however lofty, are emptied of content and become mere illusions. Love, of course, means something much more than mere sentiment, much more than token favours and perfunctory almsdeeds. Love means an interior and spiritual identification with one's brother.... Love takes one's neighbour as one's other self, and loves him with all the immense humility and discretion and reserve and reverence without which no one can presume to enter into the sanctuary of another's subjectivity.... Love demands a

complete inner transformation – for without this we cannot possibly come to identify ourselves with our brother."[69]

Merton conveys the transforming nature of relationships and recognises the costliness involved in the hard slog entailed in the development of such profound interpersonal connections. The love that Christians are called to have for one another is intensely engaging, and for this reason it also is incredibly difficult to nurture and sustain. Unlike hedonism, with the gratifying immediacy of its facile pleasures, this intimate engagement never is meant to lead to self-centredness or self-absorption. For some of us we only learn how love can mature into the unconditional selflessness of *agape* through experiencing first the passionate nature of *eros*. For my part I must confess to making plenty of mistakes along the pathway of loving and being loved. Yet through the clarity of hindsight I can see how I've benefited from participation in love because every relationship helped to point me towards God who is ultimate Love.

Eros and *agape* are not two disconnected loves. Actually they are two qualities found within our human love, and as such both of them are complementary aspects reflecting the divine love of God. My relationship with God is expressed in and through my human commitments. One might even assert that my relationship with God is "embodied" – or fleshed out – through the course and conduct of my relationships with others. As a person who now is committed to monastic celibacy these connections no longer involve physically sexual components, yet emotional intimacy remains alive and active within my close relationships. Through the incarnation God was united with the human spirit. As a result of that union the human body became the temple to be lifted up into intimacy with God. Divine *eros* is God's passionate desire to bring us into union with himself, and our bodies are active participants in this union.

Mark Vernon says that "in friendship, two intimate friends gain a glimpse of the life that awaits them in God. Friendship provides a foretaste of heaven … friendship's greatest gift is in lifting the veil between this world and the next. It provides an intimation of everlasting love."[70] Although you may consider it odd to hear me assert that I am experiencing the incredible intensity of love here

---

[69] Thomas Merton, The Wisdom of the Desert, p. 17.
[70] Mark Vernon, *One soul, two bodies.* The Tablet, 3 April 2010, p. 11.

within a monastic setting, this is indeed the reality of my life in the Community of the Resurrection.

Friendship is a risky kind of love and I know personally the difficulties of nurturing and maintaining it. But weathering the frustrations and disappointments that are a natural part of an intimate friendship definitely is worth the effort because within that relationship one receives a taste of divine love. Possessing a free will, and thus not driven merely by instincts as are some of the other species, each one of us has the choice of whether to love or not to love. When we embrace love then a tremendous force can be awakened within us because it is in embracing love that we experience life in all of its abundance.

It is a sadly diminished view of intimacy that sees it being attainable only through genital activities. Some of the most enriching experiences of intimacy actually come through friendship. Within a religious community the shared enterprise that we participate in as part of our common vocational call is one avenue by which friendships are fostered and nourished. Since we live in an environment that is characterised by a significant amount of time dedicated to silence, it is good that intimacy does not need to involve a lot of talking. There are many other ways to communicate deeply with another person. Tears shed with a friend or family member when parting, a mischievous smile at something that two persons find amusing, being embraced by another when meeting, a tender touch conveying comfort and support, or just sitting with another person: these are some examples of intimate occasions that have disclosed far more about me than my rambling words.

No one can get away entirely from relationships. Even hermits who've ventured out into the barren desert or the rugged wilderness seldom have been able to avoid all contact with another human being. Furthermore we are shaped not only by our present relationships but also by each of those from our past. Every one of us is the unique person that we are due to all of the formative relationships that have been a part of our life. Some of them have been positive and ennobled us whilst others may have been negative and saddled us with burdens that we're still carrying. None the less we are the sum of all of our relationships because they contribute to the distinctiveness of our identity.

Extroversion is not a natural part of my personality, and intimacy seldom happens instantly or easily for me. I ought to clarify this by stating that intimacy and attraction are not synonymous. There have been times when I've been attracted to someone the very first time that I caught sight of that individual, but that was a physiological response brought about through my visual interest in that person's physique. Occasionally the attraction that I've felt for someone has led me to introduce myself and engage in conversation, but most of the time my initial curiosity never progressed beyond looking at the attractive person who caught my interest. That definitely is not intimacy; it is merely the visually stimulated emotion of attraction. Unlike sex, in the purely physiological act, intimacy does not happen simply because one desires it or has a 'need' for it. Instead it is enabled by the behaviours that we choose in the course of relating to another person.

A healthy monastic community must be built upon a foundation of love. Simply existing side by side with one another in an atmosphere of cold indifference or begrudging tolerance is not enough to nourish our souls. The love that must be present neither abuses nor exploits another person. It is a love that gives gladly without requiring equal payment in return because it is not offered for the gratification of the self. Such a love should not be regarded as appropriate only for nuns and monks or other spiritually enlightened people. It really is the same love that all Christians are called by Christ to share with other people. Monastic celibacy is not loveless. It is an expression of human love that points to the much greater divine love. Celibacy challenges the sexual consumerism of our contemporary society by pointing to something enriching beyond temporary sensual pleasures and which is eternal in its satisfaction.

Saint Aelred, a twelfth-century abbot, wrote: "God is friendship.... But still what is true of love, I surely do not hesitate to grant to friendship, since he that abides in friendship, abides in God, and God in him."[71] Those words from a medieval monk remind us of how important it is not to reduce our understanding of sexuality to genital activity. This is especially difficult because the contemporary media conveys the false message that only within passionately physical and romantically arousing behaviour can intimacy and love be found. Hollywood has made a fortune from "feel good" romantic movies in which an attractive couple meet spontaneously, quickly connect physically, and then live in the blissful world of "happily ever after."

---

[71] Aelred of Rievaulx, Spiritual Friendship, p. 66.

Those films portray an unrealistic view of relationships that is a diminishment of the biblical understanding of healthy human sexuality.

In its most comprehensive sense sexuality covers the whole range of experiences of our human embodiment as it embraces all of the feelings and emotions that move us towards genuine communion with other people. Within our experiences of intimacy with others we are enabled to learn a way of being fully present to others rather than being aloof and superficial in our emotional lives. Such interactions between people do not require coitus in order to achieve a genuinely satisfying interpersonal intimacy.

There is a significant level of risk involved in engaging in intimacy because it moves us beyond the comfortable security where we alone are in control. But the rewards are worth the costliness of engaging with others. Through the experiences of spiritual communion of one person with another, truth is revealed in the process of self-disclosure and mutual sharing. Falling in love, both with another person and with God, is what makes it possible for us to surrender the "self" to any significant degree. This falling deeply into love need not involve sexual intercourse in order to have a life transforming quality to it.

Sometimes Christians think that they must choose between passionate union with another human being and a relationship of intensity and depth with God. Such a polarised choice is theologically incorrect. This "either-or" equation of choosing one love over another is not part of God's demands upon us. It is perfectly natural to long for human intimacy and to wish to know and to be fully known by someone whom we love. There is a link between humanity's desire for intimacy and God's desire for an intimate communion with us. God is indeed the divine author of passionate communion and thus he is its most determined champion, so there is no need for us to make an arbitrary choice between the love of another person and the love of God.

The author of Ecclesiastes beautifully affirms such intimacy when writing: "Two are better than one ... for if they fall, one will lift up the other ... Again, if two lie together they keep warm, but how can one keep warm alone?" It is important to notice that passage's conclusion with an emphasis upon the necessity of the divine partner being present within the relationship: "A threefold cord is not quickly broken."[72]

---

[72] Ecclesiastes 4:9-12

When I've fallen short of the vocational calling that God has laid upon my heart, my brothers have lifted me to my feet and revived the embers of my spiritual passion. It is the third cord, Jesus Christ, that binds and strengthens us in our common life. I am grateful that God always is in our midst as the foundation on which our relationships find their centre and their stability.

Some of you may have experienced the profound spiritual dimension of intimacy; of being caught up in a transcendence that goes beyond physical pleasure and emotional delight. Such opportunities offer a glimpse of a divine reality beyond ourselves, and they are a delight surpassing the physiological actions of an orgasm. Those moments are God-given occasions when we are able to draw closer to genuine communion with the divine Source of all love. Few of us mortals are permitted, or could bear, to dwell for long durations of time on such lofty spiritual heights of intimacy. Usually the veil of such transcendence parts only briefly – just long enough to glimpse the numinous. Although short in their duration, yet those brief ecstatic moments are marvellous experiences during which our consciousness is altered and we are enabled to gaze upon the sacredness of love and the miracle of life. On those occasions, as we feel the awesome presence of God, we realise that we are not alone – and I don't mean simply that there is another human body lying beside you in the bed.

Sexuality is a wonderful gift from God and it deserves to be affirmed and appreciated as fully as possible. Our choice in life always ought to be loving others, regardless of whether this is borne out through the vowed celibacy of a monastic vocation, the pledged commitment of marriage, being partnered or being single. Human fulfilment is found in cherishing and nurturing others even when the costs incurred to us are significant. We are called to love whether or not we in turn get anything lucrative out of it. It is the non-possessive, non-manipulating nurturance and acceptance of other people which makes human fulfilment possible. An example that springs to mind is the way that my parents have been unconditionally supportive of my pursuit of a monastic vocation even though they do not understand it themselves. They probably would not have selected such a counter-cultural pathway for their son's life if they'd been solely in charge of making a career decision. Despite their own anxieties about my choice to become a monk, they have exemplified a supportive, non-judgemental love reflecting the 'love regardless of the cost' demonstrated most clearly by Jesus Christ.

Personally I do not think that there is a different kind of love for married people as contrasted for those who are single and celibate. Different relationships each contain a common essence of intimacy even though the details of its physical expression will be varied. What makes these relationships intimate is the interaction between the participants allowing the personality of one to fuse with the other whilst each still remains distinct and unique. No one is dominated, abused or manipulated by coming together within the realm of genuine intimacy, and when this holistic communion with others is centred upon God then it can become a sacramental experience of transcendence. The Cistercian monk Brian McGuire writes about how this spiritual quality of intimacy was at the core of St. Aelred's understanding of friendship: "Aelred insisted on loving and being loved … and in combining everything in God and man in one complete dynamic of love…. He combined loving other men with loving God in the human and approachable Jesus to whom he reached out in his community of love."[73]

Without exception every person is a sexual being. We can either ignore and repress our sexuality or we can live positively and healthily within it. The one option that is not available is to bypass it in the vain hope of achieving an escape from it. As an integral element of our humanity it is not possible to exist divorced from our sexuality because we cannot live as disembodied entities. One of the most important tasks of spirituality is to help us understand our sexuality and how we can live within it positively and creatively. This quest for understanding and acceptance is just as essential a journey for those living within the vows of celibacy as it is for those who are married, partnered or single.

Our bodies are neither incidental nor extraneous to our spiritual formation. Our bodily selves, with all of our emotions and passions, are fundamental to our full personhood. This means that our longing for fulfilment in God cannot be based on denigrating the forms of love that connect us to other members of the human family. By drawing us into a more perfect relationship with God the highest forms of love

---

[73] Brian Patrick McGuire,
    Friendship and Community: The Monastic Experience, p. 337.

include rather than exclude the best that is found within all our experiences of love. Cornelius Wencel, a Camoldolese monk, has written the following about the dynamic interaction between human and divine love:

> "The more we are as one with Christ, and the closer and more intimate our relationship with Him becomes, the more we can learn to understand our original identity. We get to know ourselves thanks to our relations with God, the world, and other people... Love lets us know our identity, which guarantees our freedom."[74]

Even erotic desires can become a means of pointing beyond a narcissistic focus upon yourself towards the profoundly enriching unity experienced through intimate communion with another person. As long as it aspires to be a gift of the self and a joyful receiving of the other person rather than merely an exchange of bodily stimulation, then giving and receiving sexually can have a sacramental quality to it as one person's spirit touches that of another. Our deepest desires can move us beyond self-centredness to self-giving, and thereby we discover truths about the nature of God and our own place within God's great dominion.

The theological implications of the incarnation proclaim that the presence of God is found in all sorts of human experiences, not the least of which are those involving human desire and intimacy. Whether or not we live physically active sexual lives or within the vows of celibacy, a healthy balance between solitude and intimacy is vitally important for us. By our very nature as social beings the species *homo sapiens* are designed to walk through life in companionship with other people. These interpersonal interactions quite naturally will involve some degree of intimacy.

The Church cannot hope to speak effectively to society if it cannot first be honest about human sexuality! If the Church fails to do this then there is little prospect of contemporary society listening to what Christians are saying about spirituality. Whether or not we like it, the sobering fact is that society will judge us first by our attitudes towards human sexuality before pausing long enough to hear our proclamations on the subjects of faith. People might be more responsive to the Church if we put into practice these words from the First Letter of

---

[74] Cornelius Wencel, The Eremitic Life, p. 91.

John: "God is love, and those who abide in love abide in God, and God abides in them."[75]

---

[75] 1 John 4:16

Chapter 13: Totem Pole Turned Upside Down

I have several academic degrees, but all the knowledge in the world does not matter if I am not willing to give and to receive love. In my experience that is one of the hardest, and most humbling, lessons that I've ever had to learn. I am also still a novice in learning how to do this. The practice of genuine humility is difficult for most of us living in the 21st century. As an American I grew up amidst the socio-economic privileges of life in one of the world's superpowers during an era when the United States was triumphant in nearly every corner of the globe. Living in a land blessed with considerable wealth and abundant resources I felt that I was sitting easily at the top of a totem pole. I was fortunate to grow up in the comforts available to a middle-class family as a child of two educated parents who were teachers by profession. Like my peers I had been conditioned by society's messages of blatant self-promotion, and I'd internalised and come to believe those messages.

The monastic vow of obedience flies in the face of the autonomy and self-assertion that contemporary society cherishes. Nuns and monks are seeking God's kingdom, so they are not to be interested in getting their own way in matters of this earthly realm. From a culture characterised by self-serving attitudes pursued for personal pleasure, I was not gifted with an easy ability to relinquish my own agenda and desires in submission to the common will of others. Previous cultural conditioning may provide a partial explanation for my lack of humility, but it does not excuse me from the vow of obedience that still is an ongoing challenge for me.

Obedience should not be regarded merely as blind adherence to someone's arbitrary commands. To regard it in that light is to reduce it to the level of a canine obedience school. The real action of obedience takes place not on a behavioural level but in the realms of beliefs and values. It is the head and the heart, and not primarily the hands, that must learn to embrace this promise made at profession. Engaging in the struggle to grasp this vow more fully is an integral part of monastic life.

The occasional moments of exaltation found within a dramatic religious encounter with the Triune God are not the most important times in the monastic life. Wonderful as those uplifting experiences are, they seldom last for an extended length of time. Far more significant is my daily fidelity to this life that I have chosen, and much of my time and energy is involved in the effort of living faithfully for Christ each day.

People who enter the monastic life come from all manner of previous occupational pathways and bring with them a wide range of experiences. No matter how many academic credentials or pastoral accolades accompanied me on my arrival, I still entered the Community of the Resurrection at the same place as every other person who has begun this journey of discernment. Like everyone else I commenced the process as an enquirer, then became an aspirant before being admitted as a postulant, which was followed by my 'clothing' as a novice, and then later by my formal admission when I made my first profession.

Having been a lecturer at a theological college and a rector of several parishes served consecutively over the course of two decades, I was accustomed to being regarded as "the authority" by whom decisions were made and to whom deference was given. In contrast upon arriving at the monastery I had to make a dramatic change. Now I was living in a place where I was no longer the primary decision-making authority. As a rector I'd been the "top dog" presiding in my clerical collar from my perch atop the totem pole of the parochial power structure. Now the hierarchy was completely inverted, and I needed to be obedient in submitting to the will of my superiors.

I'd genuinely enjoyed my ministry as a parish priest, and sometimes I missed the public role which enabled me to feel useful to God and to my parishioners. Entering a Community whose membership is significantly geriatric I missed the greater variety of people in parish life. Baptising and marrying, preaching and teaching, visiting newborns and the homebound all provided a gratifying sense of feeling needed. When I arrived at Mirfield everything on which I had based my vocational identity and self-worth was stripped away.

I quickly discovered that as the "new guy" in this religious community everyone had seniority over me. Having to do chores such as gardening, cleaning, serving meals, washing dishes, and taking my turn at tidying up the men's urinal made it strikingly clear that my previous professional skills did not qualify me for any preferential treatment. Structuring my daily functioning according to someone else's assignment of various tasks also went against the patterns of my past when I'd been the one organising my schedule.

Every day I am learning how to conform my own will to that of God through obedience to his voice expressed through my seniors in this religious community. Obedience is not intended only for my responses to the Superior. Its practise in my life must be broader than to one individual, and slowly I am coming to appreciate being instructed by every member of this community. Each one of them has the potential to serve as an agent of God in my formation as I am learning how to live as a servant of Jesus Christ. If I am unwilling to receive advice and guidance from my monastic brethren then it is quite likely that I will miss hearing God's voice as it comes through the words and wisdom of my spiritual brothers. As another monk says, "Obedience is an antecedent openness, an attitude of receptivity, a willingness to listen combined with the recognition that this responsiveness may involve changing one's life in accordance with what one hears."[76]

Listening to God within the monastic setting is about much more than praying, studying the scriptures, and participating in the daily round of liturgies. Real spiritual listening to the 'still, small voice' of the Divine also involves hearing the advice and feedback offered by my brothers. It is one thing to receive what is directly in front of us in a text of the Bible. But it is even more challenging to expose one's ideas and aspirations to the critical voice of another person. Living in this Community I am called to seek direction from those with whom I share life in this house. Such direction comes not only from the Superior but also from all the other monks. At times they can be wise or foolish, pleasant or unbearable, erudite or naive. None the less from them come the insights that I must heed if I am to grow in my knowledge and love of God.

Throughout Saint Benedict's Rule great emphasis is placed upon submission to others, and much attention is paid to overcoming wilfulness. For me obedience to the Superior is reasonably straightforward when he is addressing matters with which I'm already in agreement and feel no need to argue. Large and weighty issue are not the only ones that challenge my obedience, and oftentimes it is in the smaller things that I find my personal submission to be most difficult. This is compounded for me when the foibles of an individual brother drive me to irritated distraction and my opposition takes on a personal note. As the Benedictine monk Mark Barrett says, "Monks

---

[76] Michael Casey, Strangers to the City, p. 92.

can be very reverential of one another in the choir, but take a look at them in the refectory."[77]

The proverbial rubber meets the road in the nitty-gritty nature of our daily interactions. Oftentimes we are polite and well-behaved within the sacred confines of the church. Then we let down our guard after the liturgy concludes and we collide, metaphorically or even literally, with another person who is in our way and inconveniencing us. In those moments, when our emotions boil over and harsh words fly, that is when our unreformed true nature shows through the pious façade that we've been wearing.

The foundation of monastic obedience lies in my willingness to give priority and pre-eminence to God's will over my own. Rendering obedience to the Superior who leads this Community is only one way by which I am imitating the self-emptying of Jesus. My acceptance of this monastic vow must move beyond my interactions with the Superior and extend wide enough to encompass listening to God speaking through any one of the brethren, the staff and volunteers, our visitors and guests, or any other member of the whole human family.

Holding back on self-assertion is a way to leave room for others so that we can hear them, and thus hear God speaking through them. Constantly I am being called to affirm others even when this has to be done at the price of not asserting my own rights or refraining from pursuing my own wishes. That is part and parcel of obedience. It has been difficult for me to do this when I've felt that more attention or deference ought to have been accorded to me. One example that I recall was my disappointment when nobody took any notice of an event that I considered significant. The occasion was the 6th May, the feast of St. John before the Latin Gate, which in 2010 marked the twentieth anniversary of my ordination. For me that was worth celebrating, but although I'd let this news be known to several others that date came and went unnoticed. In my pride I wanted to be heralded for being in holy orders for two decades. As I've grown during my monastic journey I see with greater clarity the vanity of my desire for acknowledgement and recognition. This was one small example of humility that I am learning, without which I cannot hope to arrive anywhere near the goal of obedience.

---

[77] Mark Barrett, Crossing…, p. 113.

Back at the beginning of my ordained ministry my aspirations wandered to wishful thoughts of a future elevation to some high office in the Church. This probably was not a vocational fantasy unique to me alone. I suspect that many newly ordained clergy have flirtations with dreams of lofty promotions. The passage of years has given me a clearer view of the rigours and stresses experienced by those in leadership, and now I would not want such headaches. These days I find contentment in a vocation that is not upwardly mobile. Within this small community of monastic brethren I have found enrichment, fulfilment and pleasure.

The scriptures convey examples of Jesus teaching great crowds of people, but we're also provided with illustrations of our Lord's care for individuals. In contrast to the intimacy of Christ's ministry with individuals, now we live in a culture where bigger is thought to be better and numerical growth is regarded as the most accurate measure of success. Within the spiritual economy size is not everything because substance is what really counts. Even though numbering less than twenty members, this little gathering of monks is where I find the support that nurtures me and spurs me on to further growth. It is not a steppingstone to future greatness or to ecclesiastical promotion, but this is the place where the real action is for me. Actually this *is* greatness, and I consider myself blessed to be a member of this monastic family.

Chapter 14: Could Christ Be In *Them*?

When I entered this community I could not comprehend why connecting with each of the persons around me was important. With some brothers I found myself in natural harmony. But when I was told to work with those whose methods seemed illogical or whose personalities were contrary to mine, I did not understand why it was necessary to be so involved with brothers who were incompatible with me. I also had a hard time accepting that my personal desires would not directly influence the assignment of tasks given to me. What I have discovered is that even though my relationship with God is of the utmost importance, unless it is lived out in communion with other people through love and service then I am engaged in a fruitless endeavour.

As the only son in a household with one other sibling, I had grown up in a world where I did not have to share many of my possessions. I had my own bedroom, toys and clothes and my sister had the same for herself. Most of my wishes – provided that they were not totally unreasonable – were met by my generous parents or grandparents. In some ways it seemed that the desirable things of the world belonged to me, or at least that I was entitled to a fair portion of them. The world seemed to be mine to control and shape, and within this realm of individualistic self-sufficiency I thought that I was very much an island unto myself.

In contrast to my youthful perspective, monastic spirituality proclaims that I only become a whole person when I let others into my life. Through opening my inner self my attitudes are challenged, stretched and expanded beyond the narrow confines of my limited sight. This process of growing requires constant work and it is not an easy journey. As my Superior writes, "The daily conversion of the monk or nun is a continual process in which his or her own interior climate is remade."[78]

I belong to a Community that has drawn together people of different personalities and dispositions. We belong to different generations and we have a wide variety of cultural, educational and occupational backgrounds. Throughout the time that I have lived here the membership has included people who've hailed from such globally

---

[78] George Guiver, Vision Upon Vision, p. 176.

diverse places as Bermuda, Britain, Denmark, Ireland, South Africa, and Zimbabwe, with a couple of us from the United States to complete this international mix. Our unity as brothers-in-Christ does not derive from a common national background. Instead it comes from a deliberate act of will by which each of us renounce individualism and strive to live in concord. We are one family because we have made a solemn decision to become one, and we are enabled to achieve this only through God's marvellous grace.

An ordinary affinity is not enough to hold such a collection of individuals together in mutual fidelity. Furthermore the intense closeness of shared life is a certain guarantee for each person's faults and foibles to be noticed and remarked upon by others. Something more that our noblest human intentions are necessary, and fortunately the remedy is at hand in the healing balm of God's unconditional love that covers our imperfections. Instead of the egocentric individualism and competitive approach common in much of contemporary society, here in a monastery I see more clearly how everyone is joined together and woven into one tapestry that forms the fabric of daily life.

After my last Thanksgiving holiday spent in the United States, when my parents were sad at the prospect of my relocating overseas, I told them not to look upon this as the loss of their son but rather to see it as gaining a whole community. It is reassuring for me to know that I will grow old with this monastic family around me. It isn't the same as my biological family, yet it provides a healthy way for me to live in an environment offering companionship and ministry opportunities. Our communal life is nurtured through our shared beliefs and values and our common search for union with God.

The ideals of religious life are lofty and noble. But the reality involves working constantly at seeing Christ within these brethren with whom I am living. Building community involves recognising our need for one another. Living in this collection of diverse personalities confronts me daily with my need to break down the defensive barriers that I've erected against intrusion by others. This opening of myself to them is a spiritual necessity because they are the bearers of Christ.

Tearing down my protective walls and inviting others to enter into my life challenges me because this openness must be directed towards each and every one of my monastic brothers – not just those whom I like the best. As Fr. Jeffrey, the Novice Guardian in the novel *"One Foot in Eden,"* says to a new arrival: "An elderly brother at a silent meal may be annoying because he dribbles. Someone sitting next to you in choir may drive you mad because he sings out of tune.... So don't think you have come to a monastery to have an all alone with God and escape from people."[79] When some of the brethren 'get under my skin' then irritably I ask myself, "How could Christ be in them?" The truth is that in each one of them is precisely where the Spirit of God is found. It is through my interactions with them that I am shown divine love and my need for God.

> "God manifests His presence in the world through the very sign of friendship.... A friend is "a sacrament" of God, a gift and a grace given so that the other person can be delivered and saved. A friend, through his loving, accepting and warm presence, reveals the face of God.... Selfless friendship and love in this manner become a way of realizing the deepest meaning of being human, a meeting-place of things human and things divine."[80]

Frequently society treats people as isolated and completely independent, but the monastic tradition has a different approach. This is essential because the monastic journey is not made alone. Its spirituality is communal and contains a deep sense of connectedness to every member of the human family. As such it speaks from within the language of love on the themes of unity, harmony, interrelationships and interdependence. Monastic spirituality is not meant to be remote, distant or inaccessible. It is very human and earthy, being rooted in the frail flesh of each monk or nun. Commenting upon her life in a convent, a Franciscan nun made this statement that is equally applicable to monks: "You've got to be exceptionally normal to be a nun. If you weren't, you never would survive living with people you wouldn't actually have chosen to live with. It's far from an escape, believe me. But it is a very happy life. We've got some fantastic jokers."[81]

My feelings for my monastic brothers fluctuate. Sometimes they look gifted and holy whilst at other times they seem petty and stubborn. There are occasions when life here is blissful and filled with

---

[79] Alan Wilkinson, One Foot in Eden, p. 58.

[80] Cornelius Wencel, The Eremitic Life, p. 194.

[81] Janet Fearns, interviewed by Alexandra Coghlan
The Guardian, 30 August 2010, p. 21.

pleasure, but I've also known times when this vocation seems to be nothing more than a painful cross that I must endure. Living, working, eating and worshipping alongside others whom sometimes I find irritating or inconsiderate is hard work. Our differences, and the irritation that can result, are invitations to grow in love for one another. The person who irritates me is an integral part of God's transforming me into the likeness of Christ. The scriptures call us to love our neighbours as ourselves, but that is not necessarily the same thing as liking them. Regardless of how my personality clashes with another person, yet I am called to love the Christ that is within them.

> "A community of men living and working together is not always an easy place to be. Idealism and religious devotion, good things in themselves, do not automatically produce soft edges. Interactions can be demanding and problematic ... preferring to project an image of calm and mutual friendliness, or a very English sort of politeness ... we often paper over the cracks."[82]

Outsiders observing us might think that it is a heavenly experience to live amongst a collection of professed religious. But the reality of communal life is that familiarity can breed contempt if we are not careful. It is a challenging task to perceive the holiness of the rough diamonds with whom one lives, and that is a summons which is common to every follower of Christ. It can be easier to behave in a Christ-like manner with an anonymous stranger or a mere acquaintance than in the encounters with our own family.

One morning, while I was on a retreat in Wales, I was awoken at half past four with these words audibly piercing the mists of my dreams and the fog of my sleep: "Just love me!" Shattering my slumber in a moment, those words instantly brought me to wakefulness as I heard Jesus saying "Just love me!" But how, I wondered, am I to do that? Then I realised where the battleground of loving is taking place for me. It happens right here with these brethren against whom I so often rub shoulders in the abrasive friction of life's daily interactions. "Just love me," Jesus was saying, "through Jim, Joe and Jack with whom you live." That's where the rubber meets the road – where love must be put into practice. To each one of them I am able to show my love for Jesus, but this isn't easy to do especially when I've

---

[82] Mark Barrett, Crossing..., p. 95.

been hurt by them or am angry at them. How quickly my own behaviour demonstrated this difficulty when I had a falling out with another brother soon after my return from that retreat. But love them I must because it is only through the labour of loving that I become most truly myself and most Christ-like. "Just love me!" were Jesus' words penetrating my dreamy sleep that morning. When I am loving others it is then that I am caught up into the very heart of God.

It is those who are the closest and the most intimate with us that really know how to 'push our buttons' and elicit a heated emotional reaction. But they are the ones in whom we are to see reflections of Jesus – even in our moments of anger. Through them new dimensions of God are revealed, but our mind and heart must be open if we are to be receptive to God's revelation. As Cummings says, "The astounding fact of monastic community is that in spite of our evident human brokenness and in spite of our evident personal diversity, we can live together for a lifetime with a oneness and harmony that transcend all possible expectations."[83]

This harmony does not come from an absence of conflict, and I admit that within my biological family and my monastic family there are many occasions when disagreements and conflicts arise. Yet those two families remain for me places of genuine acceptance and inner peace. My relationships with my monastic brothers are not peripheral matters to which I attend only when it's convenient. Just as with your spouse, partner, children or any others who are close to you, my monastic brothers are not people I pay attention to only after the other parts of my personal life are sorted out.

Peace is not achieved through passivity. It requires active engagement to reap the fruits of its harvest. Great effort and constant commitment are required to discern the voice of God within the person who is testing our patience and sorely trying our temper. Although monasticism places a considerable emphasis upon the individual's relationship with God, it also recognises that the vocational journey is a fruitless pursuit if not lived out in communion with other people through love. The bottom line is that our love for Christ is only as real as our love for the people around us!

In the fourth century, Evagrius Ponticus wrote a document entitled *The Praktikos* that consists of one hundred instructions addressed to

---

[83] Charles Cummings, Monastic Practices, p. 152.

monastics. This is the final one of those instructions: "It is not possible to love all the brethren to the same degree. But it is possible to associate with all in a manner that is above passion, free of resentment and hatred."[84] Due to the differences in our personalities I feel more affinity with some members of this community than with others, but for every one of them I have a deep affection. I've come to appreciate that a monastery is a school for lifelong learners where I join with my monastic brothers in striving to become more like Christ. Through the communal process of helping one another to draw closer to Jesus we are drawn closer to each other. Esther de Waal, writing about the shared nature of spirituality, states the following:

> "I shall see and find Christ in others: in the hearts and tongues and eyes and ears of all whom I meet on my journey. This is the call of St. Benedict to see all who come as Christ. It prevents any inward journey from becoming one of interior self-exploration, and instead tells me that it is one of belonging, or relationships."[85]

Much like the effort required for living within a monastic community, the spiritual life of a Christian needs to be worked at constantly. It is not something attained in an effortless manner. Building up our faith calls for discipline and mindfulness as, with deliberate intentionality, we embrace Jesus and profess ourselves ready to serve Christ. Staying put within a long-term relationship – such as marriage or a monastic profession – requires a considerable amount of stamina. It is very difficult resisting the temptation to leave when adversity arises. Within our permanent relationships we are tried and tested as our rough corners are chipped away and smoothed out through the friction that occurs whenever two objects rub together such as two persons interacting.

> "These long-term covenanted relationships at their best are windows through which God's love and calling come to us. Their longevity and covenanted quality encourage our sense of steady connectedness and care for life beyond our own. This long-term quality can also turn relationships into an ascetical arena where our hard and delusory edges are

---

[84] Evagrius Ponticus, The Praktikos, p. 41.
[85] Esther de Waal, Celtic Way of Prayer, p. 26.

exposed and worn down as we are stretched by the sheer otherness of those with whom we live."[86]

Like marriage, monastic spirituality holds up a life that goes beyond what is entirely pleasing or completely convenient for one person alone. For monks and nuns, life without the others – even when they prove to be irritating – is a life that it not really whole. Life without the obligations of attachment to these people amongst whom I am living under obedience to a monastic Rule occasionally holds the attraction of seeming easier and more free. However I realise that such freedom would prove to be a barren life for me. I am being made more whole through my association with these brothers who confront and challenge me. Walter Frere wrote in his commentary upon our Rule: "A community has a divine rather than a human unity because it rests not on natural affinities of character, association in work, or even similarity of aims, but on the divine vocation which all have been brought to share; it is this that becomes the real formative principle of the community and the compacting force of the widely various, and even divergent, elements of which it is composed."[87]

Frere's words were written in 1907 but more than a century later they still are applicable. The brethren residing at Mirfield in the 21st century are every bit as diverse as those earliest members of the Community of the Resurrection. Merely liking one another is not an adequate foundation on which to construct the edifice of unity. To be effective in sustaining a Christian community we must be committed to the same eternal things. What we live for and how we strive to live out our values are some of the central questions of community, and without a shared investment in this common understanding the Community of the Resurrection will fracture and dissolve in failure. If we rely entirely upon our own strength for the preservation of our communal life then it has no hope of success. It is the Holy Spirit that makes us one because the bonding power of love is stronger than any of the divisive forces at work in our midst.

Monastic community blossoms forth into its fullest flower in the communion of the brethren gathered around God's holy Word and partaking together of the Blessed Sacrament. Referring to the dynamic whereby the promotion of the commonweal results in benefit to

---

[86] Tilden Edwards, Spiritual Director, Spiritual Companion, p. 144.
[87] Walter Frere, A Commentary on The Rule, Chapter 9, p. 209.

individuals, Michael Casey writes, "Preferring nothing to Christ's love, each gives priority to another, and all bear one another's burdens. Oddly enough such concern for others does not issue in the annihilation of self but makes way for its flowering."[88] Through striving always to put others first the monk or nun actually is ennobled by increasingly reflecting more of Christ's light and love.

Whether within a covenanted union such as marriage or a vowed life within a religious order, we cannot love in the abstract. Noble theories and an esoteric approach are not sufficient because love must be 'fleshed out' with other people. In a religious community one quite naturally will have varying degrees of friendship with different people. These friendships, each one unique, are ways in which love takes on specificity for us. We are called to love, care for, and demonstrate concern for others – spouses, partners or monastic brethren – even when we do not feel 'in love' with them or even very friendly towards them. This requires our earnest efforts to perceive another's need and meet it according to our best abilities to give aid and succour. The biblical mandate to which all of our actions are held accountable is stated clearly in these words from the First Letter of John:

> "Beloved, let us love one another, because love is from God; everyone who loves is born of God and knows God. Whoever does not love does not know God, for God is love…. Those who say, 'I love God,' and hate their brothers and sisters are liars, for those who do not love a brother or sister whom they have seen, cannot love God whom they have not seen. The commandment we have from him is this: those who love God must love their brothers and sisters also."[89]

Taking those words to heart and living them out in daily life is a costly enterprise. No matter how difficult it is to put love into practice yet the biblical imperative sounds forth with a clarion call summoning us to love. The alternative is decidedly unattractive for anyone who desires to commune with God, because St. John did not mince any words when telling us that if we do not love then we do not know God since God is love.

---

[88] Michael Casey, Strangers to the City, p. 123.
[89] 1 John 4:7-8, 20-21

I made a commitment to love *all* the brethren of this community, both those with whom I feel goodwill and those whom I find unpleasant or incompatible with me. Accordingly I must walk in love with them through this earthly pilgrimage in times of calm as well as storms, in sickness and in health. The reality of this hit home when, within the first fortnight that I'd been back at Mirfield following the immigration dilemma that had prompted my American sojourn, three of the elderly monks had medical situations arise that necessitated their admission to the local hospital. When all is not rosy, medically or otherwise, I've still committed myself to stand in compassionate companionship with these men.

In the Calvary Garden located within our grounds there is a large crucifix. That cross is situated overlooking an escarpment facing the valley with its busy traffic on the roads and the trains running on the railway. The view in the other direction looks towards the wooden crosses in the cemetery wherein are interred those of this Community whose earthly life has ended. Much like the marriage vows in which a promise is made to walk with the other person "in sickness and in health" and "until death do us part," monks and nuns pledge themselves to one another for the duration of their earthly life. The author Graham Greene asserts that "…the only love which has lasted is the love that has accepted everything, every disappointment, every failure and every betrayal, which has accepted even the fact that in the end there is no desire so deep as the simple desire for companionship."[90] Through the vows made at profession, we commit to permanent companionship with each member of the monastic family. Personal failures and betrayals do not dissolve the bonds of this commitment. They may even work to strengthen it similar to the way in which steel is hardened in a fiery furnace.

The presence of a cemetery upon our property illustrates how monastic families live alongside their dead. The monks who are buried within this graveyard once strolled here upon the grass beneath which now they lie. They may have sat on the bench beneath the shade trees and observed how the crucifix of the Calvary Garden casts the shadow of a cross over the graves. To this peaceful place periodically I come and sit. One November morning, when the frost was heavy on the lawn and the air was crisp with an autumnal chill, I walked into the

---

[90] Graham Greene, May We Borrow Your Husband? p. 32.

Calvary Garden with a heart weighed down in distress. There I stood before the crucifix as I poured out tearful prayers to Christ.

In the cold air that morning my breath was clearly visible, and condensation had formed upon the head of Jesus. As my own tears wet my cheeks, I noticed a bead of moisture run down from Christ's forehead and fall from his cheek to the ground below. In that moment I realised that I was not alone as I was crying in despair. My Saviour was crying with me! One of the consolations of community life is that my brothers-in-Christ are here to laugh and to cry with me. When I walk between the rows of wooden crosses that mark the graves of our deceased brethren, I feel a personal connection with the communion of saints – both those that are memorialised in this cemetery and those still alive with whom I dwell in the House of the Resurrection.

In the Second Letter to Timothy the author wrote that as the time of his earthly departure was getting near at hand, "I have fought the good fight, I have finished the race, I have kept the faith."[91] That is a fair summation of the monastic life, much of which simply is persevering and keeping the faith. This must be done day in and day out, chore after chore, office after office, psalm following psalm, irrespective of one's feelings or emotions. When life seems to be a struggle as we're wrestling with ourselves, with one another, or with God, we are called to "keep on" running in the race.

This perseverance is meant for all Christians. Every one of us are called to keep pressing onwards, even in those occasions when the race looks impossible for us to navigate. We cannot make it over the hurdles or through the obstacles relying upon our own stamina, but with God all things are possible. Journeying through life in a monastic vocation has led me into deep communion with Jesus as I participate in loving my brothers-in-Christ. When they reciprocate and love me a tremendous circle of love is created within which we are joined together despite our differences.

It is relatively straightforward to be calm and even-tempered in private, and it's even rather easy to be virtuous when alone. But most people do not live in absolute isolation. An integral component of the spiritual race involves our encountering other human beings. Sometimes they bump into us as we collide and then stagger away bruised and hurting. At other times they may encourage us and hold

---

[91] 2 Timothy 4:7

our hands, pulling us along when we'd almost given up. Christian discipleship does not permit the easy escape of sitting on the side lines watching others run the race of faith. To attain the abundant life that Jesus promises we cannot run away from confronting the difficulties and the obstructions that appear in our pathways.

There is a popular misconception that becoming a monk or a nun means living as a hermit. For those of us residing in religious communities we know that this is not true. There are times when some of us wish that we were in the isolated peace of a hermitage rather than immersed within the frictions involved in living with other people. Such a flight from encountering Christ in others is not the solution. Regardless of what my personal feelings may be, the monastic vocation calls me to nurture my relationships with each one of my brothers-in-Christ.

There is an ancient axiom that says, "A solitary Christian is no Christian at all." I think that saying is trying to refute that faith is only a matter involving *"Me and Jesus."* Being a Christian requires a personal relationship with Jesus **and** it also demands relationships with those who are Christ's disciples. The crucifix in the Calvary Garden that once wept with me also shows me that Christ is in others. Upon more than one occasion, when I've stood before it talking to Jesus about a troubled relationship that I am having within the Community, I have turned my gaze upon the crucified Christ in an effort to alleviate the estrangement and alienation that I feel. Irritated by one of my monastic brethren, I've sought relief through communing directly with the Saviour. Instead I have found that the face of that statue becomes the very same face of the monastic brother with whom I am angry. At such times I would prefer simply to love Jesus alone, but instead of an individualistic communion with the Divine I've been confronted with a graphic reminder that Christ is in my neighbour.

Through our union with Christ we are united together in one body. When I am in the solitude of my room even then I am not alone. At all times I am knit together in spiritual fellowship with everyone else who is a follower of Christ. This bond of fellowship crosses the barriers of the Atlantic Ocean and reaches to my family, my friends, and the parishioners in those places where I've served as a priest. It also links me to every one of my spiritual brothers here in Mirfield. It is the relationships that I have with my brethren, and the experiences that we are sharing together, that makes this place to feel like a real home.

They are the ones who make me feel welcome, secure, comforted and accepted in this place. This is why I am able to be at peace amongst them.

Admittedly this is not always an easy peace, and occasionally the calm is disturbed and waves of disruption result that rock this communal ship on which we've all embarked. Life for Christians, both those living inside or outside a monastery, does not consist only of sailing upon placid seas. This should not come as a surprise since the scriptures do not promise a kind of peace that is within human comprehension. Instead we're told that "The peace of God, which surpasses all understanding, will guard your hearts and your minds in Christ Jesus."[92] So it won't be the type of peace that we'd have chosen if the selection had been left to our own devices. Instead God provides us with a gift of divine peace that turns out to be far better than any of the alternatives which we could have possibly imagined.

---

[92] Philippians 4:7

Chapter 15: Dying To Live

When I first arrived at the House of the Resurrection my views of this place were coloured by the lenses of a naively utopian perspective. I still observe this wide-eyed wonderment in some of the guests who come here. The reality is that this monastic community, like every other religious order, is only in the stage of becoming what it ought to be. Conformity to the image of heaven continues to be our common goal, but we're certainly nowhere near that spiritually enlightened state. However I have experienced moments in which some aspects of paradise are revealed. None the less it continues to be an ongoing journey into spiritual maturity that requires the diligence and devotion of each one of us.

Newcomers to monastic life generally are not assigned jobs or tasks that demand an enormous amount of responsibility. This is avoided deliberately so that new entrants can focus on the formative work of the novitiate. What is this work? To a large extent it involves the dismantling of the egocentric self and the birthing of the true self. This teaching goes back to Jesus who proclaimed that if we want to be disciples then it is necessary to take up the cross. Once again it comes back to the paradox of saving life by first losing it. Thomas Merton, a Trappist monk, addressed this when he wrote: "The risen life is not easy; it is also a dying life. The presence of the Resurrection in our lives means the presence of the Cross, for we do not rise with Christ unless we also first die with him."[93]

This was impressed upon me on the occasion of my forty-fifth birthday, which was the first one that I celebrated within this Community. On Saint Alban's Day, when we commemorated England's first Christian martyr, these were the words of the antiphon that was sung: "Unless a grain of wheat falls into the ground and dies, it remains alone." Those biblical words, set to the plainsong music of the chant, reminded me that my old self must die in order to be transformed into the new life which is being born in me. Inspiring me are the nail-pierced hands of Jesus which reveal the love-filled heart of God.

The liturgy of my first profession about a year and a half later contained a focus on this theme of dying to the self in order to be

---

[93] Thomas Merton, He is Risen, p. 18.

resurrected to living fully. There in the church, kneeling before the altar, I put myself at the disposal of this group of men living here in Mirfield. In my profession vows I surrendered my independence and placed myself under obedience. This was a prospect that I'd found intimidating when contemplating it during my pre-profession retreat with the Anglican nuns at the Convent of the Holy Name. With trepidation I realised that I was placing myself in the hands of others who would become integral parts of every major decision for the rest of my life. Essentially I was publicly announcing this: "I am not an independent entity unto myself."

To my joy I have discovered that placing myself in the hands of others has led to being embraced by them in love. The mutuality of our commitment was driven home in a powerful way during the Night Vigil immediately before the Mass in which I made my first profession. All through the night I sat in the Resurrection Chapel in a prayer vigil, but I was never alone during those long hours of darkness between 9 o'clock in the evening and 7:30 the next morning. My brothers in this Community each sacrificed some of their own sleep to spend time in shifts of one or more hours sitting with me in the shared intimacy of our silent prayer. Voicing my commitment to this Community in those vows has helped me to cast aside my attachment to the idol of self-sufficiency. It is a great relief resting on the support of these brethren whose love for me is shown by their words but even more importantly by their actions.

Our habit, consisting of a black cassock and a grey scapular, could be considered as symbolising the death to the world involved in a person's entrance into a religious community. No longer do we stroll around town clothed in the latest styles for we have died to contemporary fashion. The simple garb that is shared as the common 'uniform' of the Community is our normative apparel. Every person on earth has a unique vocational journey. For me entering a religious community was a step on the lifelong pilgrimage of faith that each Christian commences at their baptism. Although our monastic attire makes us look different from most other people, the bottom line is that the heart of my vocation really is the same as that of any Christian. All who are followers of Christ are called to enter more deeply into union with the God who loves us. As disciples of our Lord that is something we all share regardless of what we wear or where we live.

Having acknowledged a vocational commonality between those inside a monastery and the larger body of Christians who do not live within a cloister, in all fairness you might ask this: "If we're all travelling on a common faith journey, then why resort to a monastery? Why enter that kind of life and give up so much?" I'd say that what meets one person's spiritual needs is not always going to work for another person. We each must find the environment that is right for us. I also believe that by practising disciplined restraint instead of pursuing my own gratification I am enabled to overcome my weakness and live into the fullness of the abundant life intended by Christ. Learning to be more cooperative and less competitive, and working for the collective good rather than for my personal welfare, are difficult pathways for me to navigate. Like all humans I am innately self-centred. I also struggle daily with being loving. Monasticism strives to counter these traits. One reason that I find this life so rewarding is because of the correctives within its traditions that moderate my personality and mature my character.

Self-realisation for a monk or a nun is not a narcissistic pursuit. It arises from fidelity to God's call embodied in who we are as humans, as Christians, and as professed religious. In the words of an anonymous Carthusian monk: "To put Christ at the centre of everything, to see everything in relation to him, to love and to act in the light of this perspective, involves a death to self and a deep transformation of one's heart."[94] This death to self, with its accompanying transformation of the heart, never is an easy process. None the less the painful efforts are worthwhile because of the glorious resurrection that results from the journey. There is a costliness to this self-sacrifice by which we lose ourselves in order to gain eternal life.

Two things that are at the centre of every Christian's spiritual journey are emptiness and love. The question for each one of us is this: "Do we dare to risk the emptiness in order to receive the love?" In the Benedictine tradition aspects of dying to self are contained within the vow of 'conversion of life.' This is not a one-time occurrence, and a nun or monk never achieves completely such an ennobled status whilst walking through this earthly life. Rather this *'conversio'* of which Saint Benedict writes entails striving continually for conversion into a person more clearly reflecting the light of Christ.

---

[94] The Wound of Love, p. 71.

A monastic makes this effort in order to become more closely conformed to what God wants one to be. As Mark Barrett states, "The growth in wisdom which monastic life, like any spiritual path, is supposed to create should set us free to change and be changed. Stasis creates fossils, but only the dynamism of love creates human beings."[95] This holistic conversion of one's life can happen only within the context of love, and that is what every good religious order should have at its centre since it enables the creation of a fully authenticated human being.

I can attest to love being rooted firmly at the centre of this particular Community of which I am a member. These monks who are my brothers-in-Christ are not unloving, world-rejecting, body-denying people. Instead I've found them to be gentle, tolerant, wise and loving towards themselves, to me, and to our guests. It is not true that the monastic vocation is a joyless and loveless lifestyle. Although someone who sees the lives of nuns and monks as a sexless existence may be surprised by the following assertion, I want to say emphatically that it is within the monastic life that I am learning how to love.

Within this monastery my narcissism and preoccupation with self are giving way to empathy and self-giving. This process of learning how to love better is very difficult, and these insights only are attained over the course of time's passing and with the expenditure of considerable effort against my ingrained resistance. The journey into genuine love involves a never-ending transformation as the old self is made, bit by painful bit, into a spiritually new person. This is the resurrection for us – not merely a single event but rather an ongoing process in which we are engaged for our entire lives. Like all other Christians, nuns and monks are striving – and struggling – to become more like Jesus Christ. With conciseness Abbot Paul Delatte conveys this continual quest to become more Christ like, which is an aspiration that ought to be shared by every one of the Messiah's disciples:

> "The imitation of our Lord consists … of lending ourselves with flexibility to the living influence of the Lord who is within us, in such a way that our activity is a continuous translation or expression of the life of the Lord within us."[96]

---

[95] Mark Barrett, Crossing …, p. 103.
[96] Paul Delatte, The Rule of Saint Benedict: A Commentary, p.23

Chapter 16: Going Into Deep Water

The Bible proclaims that "God is love" and that by our creation we are made in the image of God. Therefore it is appropriate to say that we are made in the image of Love, which is the reason for our existence. The journey into love, which is common to all of humanity, can go badly astray when the ultimate object of the quest is lost to our sight. This happens when the search for love forgets the divine Source of all love and loses intimate contact with the incarnate Son of God who, in the words of a famous hymn, is the "love divine, all loves excelling."

Having lost touch with the miraculous and the supernatural, our contemporary society has become increasingly internalised and individualised in its quest for affirmation, fulfilment and salvation. Even the Church is regarded by many 21st century people as merely another consumer oriented organisation, one amongst many other skilfully advertised competitors whose reason for existence is thought to be primarily for encouraging individual fulfilment and providing personal satisfaction.

I observed this a-la-carte approach to Christianity at the celebration of the Eucharist on All Saints' Day held in the theatre of the *QE2* when I made a transatlantic crossing aboard that vessel. In the ship's *'Daily Programme'* the celebration of that holy day was only one item featured in a lengthy list of so-called "entertainment" options offered for the pleasure of the passengers. There were many other choices competing with the Anglican liturgy, and judging by the small number of people present I think that most people found the other choices to be more attractive and entertaining. What they missed on that All Saints' Day was the opportunity to be nourished by the sacramental Body of Christ so that they could be transformed into the corporate Body of Christ. People in our contemporary world seem to hunger for a sense of community, yet by failing to attend the Mass those other passengers missed an opportunity to commune with Christ and with his disciples.

We live in a world that is crowded yet remains full of people who are strangers to us. Modern society suffers from an estrangement with its past, its culture and its spiritual heritage. Frequently people are estranged from their neighbours, from family and friends, from their own inner self, and from God. Christians would have to be blind not to observe the painful searching being done by society's wounded and alienated people seeking genuinely hospitable places wherein life can be lived in a nurturing community. What are Christians to do about this? After prayerful discernment each of you must answer that question for yourselves. The course chosen will not be the same for everyone. You must discern how best to make yourselves available for God's service. For me the personal response that seemed most appropriate is a monastic vocation.

In a gospel passage Jesus tells some Galilean fishermen to "Put out into deep water and let down your nets for a catch."[97] Jesus is challenging them to push out further into the deeper water in order to see what happens. We have a tendency to shy away from venturing into the uncharted darkness of deep water. Instead we prefer to stay close to the shore, where things look familiar and life seems more manageable. Perhaps we feel safer with the shoreline in sight, because that visual prospect gives us a fairly accessible escape route if the sea gets rough and we want to return to the security of dry land.

I recoil at the thought of doing something different if it propels me beyond the boundaries of my ordinary patterns of functioning. Anxiety arises at the thought of going into anything new. I prefer to stay put right where I am, even if it means staying in my current "rut" that might be dull and lifeless but whose routines feel safe because they are predictable. Whenever the conventional wisdom is put forward to protect the status quo by proclaiming the futility of journeying forth into the deep waters of the unknown, then I latch onto that as an excuse to avoid a new venture.

The Galilean fishermen to whom Jesus spoke had been working all night long. They were exhausted from their labours and discouraged by their lack of success. When I feel that way I respond to God's promptings with moans and complaints as I exclaim: "I'm too tired to do that today." In this way I postpone pursuing the project to which God is calling me. Deep down I hope that my procrastination will result in the unwanted project's eventual abandonment because that would relieve me of the responsibility to pursue it in the future.

When we take the risk of going into the deep waters then we become instruments of God participating in the abundant harvest that is provided by our bountiful Sovereign. This entails going out into life's stormy seas so that we can take part in the transformation of the world.

---

[97] Luke 5:4

In the process we risk our own comfort and security for the sake of promoting the gospel values of love, compassion, justice and reconciliation. Ironically through such self-sacrificing actions we can experience a profound sense of peace even whilst being buffeted by the high waves of a storm.

As a markedly counter-cultural lifestyle, monasticism was the 'deep water' into which I felt that God was calling me to venture. I did not enter this Community for the purpose of retreating from the world or escaping from it. If I had come with that intention then quite quickly I would have realised that impossibility. Within a monastery the trials and tribulations of the world are very much alive and active. I came here to test my vocation knowing that the experience would not always be a plush and fragrant bed of rose petals. I've had to let go of the cherished items and comfortable patterns of life I'd known for the previous four decades. This painful relinquishing was necessary for cultivating the inner stillness that enables me to hear God.

The monastic vocation is a life-long journey to God that is possible only because it is a journey being done *with* God. It is the search for the Lover of our souls who already knew us long before we had our first thought of beginning the search. It is important to be clear that the pursuit of a monastic vocation is not primarily about the individual who is engaging in it. That would be a narcissistic endeavour not in harmony with the monastic ethos whose focus is on other persons and especially on the divine Other. In reference to this non-egocentric focus, Michael Casey asserts that "Christian monasticism is not a system of spiritual self-improvement; it is a means that some people need to sustain and deepen their relationship to Christ."[98] Do not admire me for pursuing a vowed life that embraces poverty, celibacy and obedience. It was due to my inability in living Christianity on my own that I sought the support of a community to nurture and sustain me in my faith journey.

Whenever one senses a call from God the only thing to do is to test it. That is scary because it means asking questions whose answers may be unsettling. But those questions challenge our growth into the fullness of the fruitful life that God desires for us. The monastic life has proven to be unsettling and upsetting to some aspects of my personality, but it is offering me a pathway of purifying my heart so

---

[98] Michael Casey, Strangers to the City, p. 142.

that I can better receive the awesome mystery of God. Daily I am being offered opportunities to fall more deeply in love with God, and nothing on earth can compare with the richness of this intimacy that satisfies my innermost longings.

Even though Mirfield is many miles from my natal land, entering the Community of the Resurrection has been a spiritual homecoming for me. There have been plenty of times when I've felt like a stranger from another world who has been dropped down in a foreign land. Rowan Williams, commenting upon some themes of the book of *Genesis*, writes that the Bible's first book "hints very strongly that life as a human being ... is a life where growth always means a step beyond what is familiar; a step away from home; that 'exile' is a state of being for us."[99] There are elements of 'exile' and of a storm-tossed 'deep water' experience for all of us when we are living as disciples of Jesus Christ. This is true whether your residence is within a monastery or somewhere else.

Hearkening back to the gospel account of boats on the Sea of Galilee brings me to the thought that we all are travelling in one boat. Obviously you cannot push that analogy too far because it is preposterous to imagine a boat large enough to accommodate so many millions of Christians. But the point in the analogy is that I cannot set out seeking God as if I am the only person on board. The pathway to wholeness, and to holiness, is amongst the throng of other travellers who also have embarked upon this voyage that is the pilgrimage of faith. I am glad that the brethren of the Community of the Resurrection invited me aboard their boat to accompany them on a journey of seeking God.

No monastic community is guaranteed to be on-track in its navigational accuracy in journeying towards union with Christ. Constant efforts must be made to ensure that the values of the Kingdom of God remain firmly rooted at its core. Compassion, mercy, forgiveness and reconciliation are not attributes automatically manifest in the behaviour of nuns or monks. How easily the less-than-attractive aspects of our unreformed human nature show up and reveal the selfishness that resides within each of us.

It is possible for me to be a monk who goes to chapel for all of the liturgies but doesn't remember that the purpose of reading the Gospel

---

[99] Rowan Williams, For All That Has Been, Thanks, p. 84.

is to become a person who reflects its values. Equally a Christian can attend church every Sunday of the year but neglect living out the Gospel heard week after week. The goal that nuns and monks share with all Christians is to become more like the Christ whom we worship. Every disciple should desire to be transformed into a person whose entire life shows forth the glory of God. To do otherwise, no matter how devout our attendance at church, will result in developing into something that is little more than a static fixture without the animating spirit of love – hardly better than a piece of furniture such as the pew that one occupies.

Everyone who becomes a follower of Jesus is called to move from their old nature into a new one, so I am not alone in having been called out of my former life into a new lifestyle. You may not feel that God is prompting you to become a nun or a monk, but like me you are called to engage in the process of being transformed by the Saviour's love into a new creation. My personal response to this requires faithfulness to my monastic brothers as I am growing into understanding the breadth and the depth of communion that we have with each other through Christ. Even though I have dwelt here since the autumn of 2009, and now have taken the vows of first profession, each day I am discovering new insights about the life of faith through living amongst my brothers-in-Christ.

The collect for religious orders from *The Book of Common Prayer* contains these words: "Guide and sanctify, we pray, those whom you call to follow you under the vows of poverty, chastity, and obedience, that by their prayer and service they may enrich the Church, and by their life and worship may glorify your Name."[100] That prayer expresses my view that this monastic vocation is not merely self-serving. I do not want this spiritual journey within the 'cloister' to be gratifying and satisfying only for my spiritual desires and longings. Instead my hope is that my monastic vocation may be a means by which I am enabled to serve and enrich the whole Church of God.

A similar sentiment to that quoted above is found in the collect for religious communities within the *South African Prayer Book*. A portion of that prayer says "Call many to Religious Communities that, waiting upon you in contemplation, they may share with others what

---

[100] The Book of Common Prayer (USA 1979), p. 819.

111

they have received from you."[101] That prayer emphasizes sharing the gifts of the monastic life with others. Living within a community whose day is structured around the contemplation and worship of God is a great gift, but nuns and monks would possess an inadequate understanding of stewardship if they did not share themselves with others. This vowed life does not exist merely to provide profoundly moving spiritual encounters that are limited exclusively to those wearing habits. Our task is to share the gifts that we receive from God with those around us.

The gospels call us to offer ourselves as missionaries: as people whose lives portray to others the compassionate love that Jesus demonstrated throughout his earthly ministry. Following our Lord's model of self-sacrificing service rendered to others is a mandate given to all disciples. Giving ourselves in service to another takes us out of our own notions of who we are. It takes us into the deep waters of unfamiliar territory where we enter another person's environment. In this way we are challenged by moving beyond the cosy territory of our personal comfort zones, and this enables us to meet others wherever they are rather than expecting them to come to us on our turf.

If we have internalised the gospel's lessons then we will heed God's call to live a life characterised by missionary service and unconditional caring. It is a life in which the old self is discarded, albeit step by painful step, whilst a new self is birthed. Through the compassionate ministries in which we engage and offer ourselves to others we are being transformed. From personal experience I can attest that one does not participate in ministry without being changed in the process – and this applies to the myriad varieties of Christian service participated in by ordained and lay people.

Since God's call is something shared in common by all of us, we need to see ourselves as part of a larger body in order to understand the gospel mandate to live out an active missionary ministry within our daily lives. The monks of the Community of the Resurrection recognise the importance of this common vocation that is shared by all Christians: "At its root, the life of the members of the Community is that of all the baptised; it is the life of the disciples of Jesus Christ. Our particular call is to live this out in community."[102] All you need to do is

---

[101] South African Prayer Book (1989), p. 85.
[102] The Community of the Resurrection, undated brochure, p. 2.

to look at the people of the world and you'll see ample evidence of their struggles with addictions, depression, disease, poverty, malnutrition, unemployment and discrimination. Not only do the poor continue to get poorer year by year, but their numbers are increasing. The mission fields surround us and we cannot escape noticing if we are attentive to the Spirit.

Jesus challenges us to take other people into consideration before we set about meeting our own needs and desires. John Donne famously said that none of us is an island, yet how often we insist on living our own comfortable lives mindless of the neediness of others around us. We act as though we are islands insulated from the harsh living conditions and the stark realities of those who are less fortunate than us.

One way by which we enter into the obedience of Christian servanthood is in surrendering ourselves to minister to the poor, the outcast and the oppressed. These people aren't only found in some exotic foreign locale like the jungles of the Amazon or the deserts of the Sahara. The simple fact is that people who are in need can be found upon our doorsteps – quite literally they may be looking at us from within our own neighbourhoods.

Through offering ourselves in Christian service to others we encounter the life transforming biblical principle that can change our lives: it is in dying that we live! It sounds contradictory yet within that paradoxical statement is a profound truth that makes life satisfying and worthwhile. As our lives are broken open and shared with others, a part of us will die.

Taking up the cross to walk as a disciple of Jesus in a monastic vocation has not been easy for me. Not one day passes without experiencing a deep ache for my family who live on another continent across the expanse of an ocean that separates us. Following the call that God placed upon my heart has not taken away my longing to be held in the arms of my loved ones. But even though the pain of our separation weighs upon me, yet I have the assurance of knowing that I am walking on the pathway to which God has called me. Some days I have felt that dying in order to live hurts too much for me to continue this journey. But I am discovering that through the sacrificial sharing of myself the process of growth into new life begins. That really is genuine living. Indeed this is what the good life is all about.

113

My personal response to our Lord's summons involved travelling overseas, entering the Community of the Resurrection, and taking up residence with the members of this Anglican religious order. That has been my own particular journey. Your spiritual journey will not be identical to mine because you are unique and your walk of faith will reflect your own individuality. None the less even though I am a monk and you probably are not, there still is much that we share in common.

Regardless of whether you are married, partnered or single, male or female, gay or straight, black or white, rich or poor – we all have a little bit of the monastic vocation inside of us. It is that interior part of our humanity that most nearly touches divinity: the part of oneself that is accessible to God alone. Every Christian's spiritual pilgrimage through life has at least a hint of monasticism flavouring it, because essentially being a nun or a monk is striving to live faithfully as a disciple of Jesus Christ. Surely that is something shared as an aspiration by all Christians?

This book has been about the search for a spiritual home. Sometimes my journey has involved aimless wandering upon various detours as I pursued distractions that seemed to promise fulfilment but eventually proved to be hollow and unrewarding. At other times I have been more responsive to God's direction and walked upon the narrow pathway leading towards salvation. Throughout all of my journeys through these four and a half decades of life, I have been driven by the desire to come home in the fullest and most real sense possible.

At the foundation of religious life is an earnest and passionate longing for home, but not simply for a place to live but for the feeling of being fully and completely "at home" within the One who is Love. This entails a sense of belonging and being loved, and it can come only from being truly at home with the Lord who has made his home within me. The monastic vocation is not an easy pathway on which to trod, but as St. Benedict says at the end of the Prologue in his <u>Rule</u> that is a foundational document for western monasticism, "as we progress in this way of life and in faith, we shall run on the path of God's commandments, our hearts overflowing with the inexpressible delight of love."[103] It is God, who is Love, that causes my heart to experience this inexpressible delight.

---

[103] Benedict of Nursia. The Rule of St. Benedict, p. 19.

Now I can say with certainty that I have found my way home. The surprise that awaited me was the realisation that the home for which my heart was searching was not to be found either in America or in England. Nor was it to be found with my biological family or my adopted monastic family. Those places and people are very dear to me, and I cherish them and hold them in my deepest affections, but even my love for them cannot make them serve effectively as a real 'soul home' for me. So where did I find my heart's home?

The answer to that question is stated by Saint Augustine of Hippo who, near the beginning of his autobiographical *Confessions*, wrote: "...because you have made us for yourself, our heart is restless until it rests in you."[104] There, with God, is my true home! My restless wandering could not cease until I realised that my much-desired 'home' always would remain inadequate if I kept looking for it to be in a particular place instead of in the divine Someone.

My restless heart remained unsettled and unsatisfied way until lodged within the Holy One who created me. As the Augustinian friar Martin Laird states, "God is our homeland. And the homing instinct of the human being is homed on God."[105] My ultimate home, which is the destination of all baptised members of the Body of Christ, is the heavenly life with God. My quest in search of this goal frequently eluded me. It did not come to consummation until I accepted that home was not going to be found in a specific geographical locale. The 'destination' is within the intimacy of a relationship with God, for there alone is it possible to find genuine peace and complete rest. In the moment when I lowered my barriers of resistance, and surrendered to falling completely into the loving arms of the Saviour, that is when I knew without a doubt that at long last I had found my heart's true home.

---

[104] St. Augustine, Confessions, Book I, p. 3
[105] Martin Laird, Into the Silent Land, p. 2.

Bibliography of Works Cited

Aelred of Rievaulx, translated by Mary Eugenia Laker, 1977, *Spiritual Friendship*, Kalamazoo: Cistercian Publications.

An Anglican Prayer Book, 1989, Church of the Province of Southern Africa, London: Collins Liturgical Publications.

Anglican Religious Life: 2010-2011, Norwich: Canterbury Press.

Anson, Peter F., 1955, *The Call of the Cloister*, London: SPCK.

Atwell, Robert, editor, 2004, *Celebrating the Saints: Daily Spiritual Readings*, Norwich: Canterbury Press.

Augustine of Hippo, translated by Henry Chadwick, 1991, *Confessions*, Oxford: Oxford University Press.

Barrett, Mark, 2001, *Crossing: Reclaiming the Landscape of our Lives*, Harrisburg: Morehouse Publishing.

Benedict of Nursia, edited by Timothy Fry, 1982, *The Rule of St. Benedict in English*, Collegeville:The Liturgical Press.

Berk, Dennis B. A.,unpublished letter September 2009.

Bona, Guerria de, 2007, *Praying with the Benedictines: A Window on the Cloister*, New York: Paulist Press.

Casey, Michael, 2005, *Strangers to the City: Reflections on the Beliefs and Values of the Rule of Saint Benedict*, Massachusetts: Paraclete Press.

Catherine of Siena, 1980, *Dialogue*, London: SPCK.

Coghlan, Alexandra, 2010, *Nun Janet Fearns on Sister Act*, *The Guardian*, Monday 30 August 2010, London, England.

Constitutions of the Community of the Resurrection, 1990, Mirfield, England.

Cray, Graham, editor, 2010, *New Monasticism as Fresh Expression of Church*, Norwich: Canterbury Press.

Crowder, Bill, 2010, *Retreating Forward* in *Our Daily Bread,* Vol. 55, Grand Rapids: RBD Ministries.

Cummings, Charles, 1986, *Monastic Practices*, Kalamazoo: Cistercian Publications.

Delatte, Paul, translator Justin McCann, 1950, The Rule of Saint Benedict: A Commentary, London: Burns and Oates.

Edwards, Tilden, 2001, *Spiritual Director, Spiritual Companion*, New York: Paulist Press.

Forrest, S.J., 1968, *Parson's Play-pen*, London: A.R. Mowbray & Company.

Franciscan Poverty: St. Francis and his Lady Poverty in *The Anglican Digest*, 2010, Vol. 52, No. 2, Arkansas: SPEAK.

116

Frere, Walter, 1907, *A Commentary on The Rule*, Mirfield:
The Community of the Resurrection.

Gaither, Gloria and Bill George, 1984, *Broken and Spilled Out,*
U.S.A.: Gaither Music Company.

Garvey, John, editor, 1988, *Circles of Love: Daily Readings with Henri J. M.
Nouwen*, London: Darton, Longman and Todd.

Greene, Graham, 1967, *May We Borrow Your Husband? and Other Comedies
of the Sexual Life*, London: The Bodley Head.

Guiver, George, 2009, *Vision Upon Vision*, Norwich: Canterbury Press.

Holden, Simon, 1982, *Ways of Praying*, Mirfield: Mirfield Publications.

Holleran, Andrew, 1996, *The Beauty of Men*, London: Picador.

Holy Bible, New Revised Standard Version, 1993,
Grand Rapids: Zondervan Bible Publishers.

Huntington, James Otis Sargent, 1996, *The Rule of James Otis Sargent and
his Successors*, New York: Order of the Holy Cross.

Israel, Martin, 1990, *Night Thoughts*, London: SPCK.

Johns, Laurentia, editor, 2008, *Touched By God: Ten Monastic Journeys*,
London: Burns and Oates.

Laird, Martin, 2006, *Into the Silent Land: The Practice of Contemplation*,
London: Darton, Longman and Todd.

Leclercq, Jean, 1974, *The Love of Learning and the Desire for God:
A Study of Monastic Culture*, Second Revised Edition, London: SPCK.

Levi, Peter, 1987, *The Frontiers of Paradise: A Study of Monks and
Monasteries*, New York: Weidenfeld and Nicolson.

Lew, Lawrence, 2010, *A Journey into Religious Life* article in *Religious Life
Review*, Vol. 49, No. 262, May/June 2010, Dublin: Dominican Publications.

Link, Julie Ackerman, 2010, *Keeping Busy?* article of 4 October 2010 in
Our Daily Bread, Grand Rapids: RBD Ministries.

McGuire, Brian Patrick, 1998, *Friendship and Community:
The Monastic Experience,* Kalamazoo: Cistercian Publications.

Merton, Thomas, 1960, *The Wisdom of the Desert: sayings of the Desert
Fathers of the Fourth Century*, London: Sheldon Press.

Merton, Thomas, 1975, *He is Risen*, Illinois: Argus Communications.

Mikes, George, 1946, *How To Be An Alien*, London: Andre Deutsch Ltd.

Mizelle, Charles, 2009, article in *Mundi Medicina*,
Vol. XXI, No. 3, New York: Holy Cross Monastery.

Mudge, Bede Thomas, 2009, article in *Mundi Medicina*,
Vol. XXI, No. 2, New York: Holy Cross Monastery.

117

Northcott, Hubert, 1955, *A Commentary on The Rule*,
Wakefield: West Yorkshire Printing.

Nouwen, Henri J.M., 1974, *Out of Solitude: Three Meditations on the
Christian Life*, Indiana: Ave Maria Press.

Nouwen, Henri J.M., 1975, *Reaching Out*, London: Harper Collins.

Nouwen, Henri J.M., 1996, *The Inner Voice of Love: A Journey through
Anguish to Freedom*, London: Darton, Longman and Todd.

Pleva, Hildegard, 2010, article in *Mundi Medicina*, Vol. XXII, No. 1,
New York: Holy Cross Monastery.

Ponticus, Evagrius, translated by John Bamberger, 1981, *The Praktikos and
Chapters on Prayer*, Kalamazoo: Cistercian Publications.

Roger of Taizé, 1965, *The Rule of Taizé*, Taizé: Les Presses de Taizé.

Roger of Taizé, 2003, *God Is Love Alone*, London: Continuum.

Siena, Biana da, 2001, *Come down, O Love divine* in
The New English Hymnal, Norwich: Canterbury Press.

The Book of Common Prayer, 1979, The Episcopal Church in the U.S.A.,
New York: Seabury Press.

The Community of the Resurrection, a brochure designed by Brian Hickling,
Mirfield: Regent Printing.

The Eucharist, a brochure by the Benedictine nuns of West Malling, England.

The Wound of Love: A Carthusian Miscellany, 1994,
London: Darton, Longman and Todd.

Vanier, Jean, 1998, *Becoming Human*, London: Darton, Longman and Todd.

Vernon, Mark, 2010, *One Soul, Two Bodies* in *The Tablet*, 3 April 2010,
London: The Tablet Publishing.

Vogue, Adalbert de, 1983, *The Rule of St. Benedict: A Doctrinal and Spiritual
Commentary*, Kalamazoo: Cistercian Publications.

Waal, Esther de, 1997, *The Celtic Way of Prayer*, New York: Image Books.

Wencel, Cornelius, 2007, *The Eremitic Life: Encountering God in Silence and
Solitude*, Ohio: Ercam Editions.

Wilkinson, Alan, 2011, *One Foot In Eden*, Mirfield: Mirfield Publications.

William, Rowen and Joan Chittister, 2010, *For All That Has Been, Thanks*,
Norwich: Canterbury Press.

Willoughby, William, 2010, *Prayer* in *The Anglican Digest*,
Vol. 52, No. 2, Arkansas: SPEAK.

Wright, Tom, 2009, *Three Lessons for Ordinands* in *The Anglican Digest*,
Vol. 51, No. 5, Arkansas: SPEAK.